ON THE OUTSIDE

Dr Guy Johnson is a Post-Doctoral Research Fellow at the Australian Housing and Urban Research Institute, RMIT University. Dr Hellene Gronda, former Research Coordinator at HomeGround Services, works for the Australian Housing and Urban Research Institute. Sally Coutts is the Manager, Research and Program Development, The Salvation Army Crisis Services.

ON THE OUTSIDE
PATHWAYS IN AND OUT OF HOMELESSNESS

BY
GUY JOHNSON
HELLENE GRONDA
SALLY COUTTS

AUSTRALIAN SCHOLARLY PUBLISHING

© Guy Johnson, Hellene Gronda & Sally Coutts 2008

First published 2008
Australian Scholarly Publishing PTY LTD
7 Lt Lothian St Nth, North Melbourne, Vic 3051
TEL: 03 9329 6963 FAX: 03 9329 5452
EMAIL: aspic@ozemail.com.au
WEB: www.scholarly.info

A Cataloguing-in-Publication entry for this title is available
from the National Library of Australia.

ISBN 978 1 74097 186 7

Copyediting by Rosemary Newman
Design and typesetting by Adam Bextream
Printing and binding by McPherson's Printing Group
Cover illustration *Heal thyself* by Tanya Ungeri

CONTENTS

Contents

ACKNOWLEDGEMENTS

Thank you to the homeless and formerly homeless people who participated in the study. Their willingness to share their experiences provided us with moving and compelling accounts. It is hoped that these accounts help to increase understanding of their situation.

Thank you to the staff at RMIT University, WAYSS Ltd (Dandenong), HomeGround Services, The Salvation Army Crisis Services (St Kilda) and The Salvation Army Social Housing Services in Leongatha and Geelong who encouraged people to participate in the interviews. Without their assistance this book would not have been possible.

Thank you to Tanya Ungeri for the front cover image and to the staff at the Public Interest Law Clearing House (PILCH) for helping to arrange it.

FOREWORD

This book is a valuable addition to our understanding of homelessness, its complex and interconnected causes and our capacity to respond with services appropriately designed and effectively delivered.

Twenty years ago, when I launched an inquiry into the plight of homeless children in Australia, many were unaware of the dimensions of homelessness in our community and of the marginalisation, discrimination and sometimes victimisation suffered by homeless people, both young and old. We can no longer plead ignorance.

However, in the last two decades our responses have been inadequate – in terms of policies and service delivery. It is encouraging that the Federal Government has committed to giving this issue priority on our social agenda. Our responses will be more successful if the research and analysis in this book are taken into account. I particularly welcome the emphasis the authors have placed on early intervention and prevention, including the still inadequately addressed challenge of mental illness, as well as the need for appropriate support to those becoming homeless through different 'pathways'.

Fortunately in the last twenty years we have developed a more mature understanding of human rights, including a recognition that the right to adequate shelter is a fundamental right, without which most other human rights lose all meaning.

We are now much richer than we were in the 1980s – economically at least – but homelessness persists and many of the most vulnerable and disadvantaged of our fellow Australians are among the homeless population. The authors clearly demonstrate the complexity of the issues associated with homelessness, but equally clearly identify poverty and extremely limited housing options as the most prevalent problems homeless people of all ages in Australia have to deal with.

Federal, state and local governments all have important roles to play in finding solutions that are based on everyone's right to live with dignity. Each of us can also find ways, however modest, to support those caring for our homeless compatriots.

Professor Brian Burdekin (AO)
Former Federal Commissioner for Human Rights

When you are approaching poverty ... you also discover the great redeeming feature of poverty: the fact that it annihilates the future.

George Orwell, *Down and Out in Paris and London*

Anyone who has ever struggled with poverty knows how extremely expensive it is to be poor.

James A Baldwin

INTRODUCTION

After all a homeless man has reason to cry, everything in the world is pointed against him.

Jack Kerouac, *The Dharma Bums*

Homelessness in Australia has changed over the last 20 years. These changes were first noted in the late 1970s when it became clear that the homeless population was becoming more diverse and was no longer a problem confined to the 'derelicts and bag ladies' of skid row. In Australia, as in the US and the UK, more young people, women and families experience homelessness than ever before.

Homelessness remains deeply entrenched in Australia's social landscape despite receiving considerable academic and government attention. Research on homelessness has proliferated since the 1980s, and federal and state governments spend hundreds of millions of dollars each year to 'address' homelessness. On census night in 2001 the Australian Bureau of Statistics estimated that 100,000 people were homeless[1]. What concerns many people is that high levels of homelessness have persisted during a period of sustained economic growth, and many people are getting trapped in a cycle, either unable to secure a home for themselves, or slipping back into homelessness repeatedly.

Although the media and the public have displayed a strong interest in homelessness over the last two decades, most people live far removed from the world of the homeless. As a result they often harbour misconceptions about homelessness that emerge in public debate. Typically discussion focuses on who or what is at 'fault'.

On one side of the debate is the enduring public perception that the homeless themselves are to blame for their plight. In a recent study examining public perceptions of homelessness, 74 per cent believed that poor decision making was the main reason people found themselves homeless[2]. This 'individualistic' perspective echoes themes of the 'undeserving' poor that emerged in England over 700 years ago.

On the other side of the debate are the advocates and agencies that blame governments for failing to ensure adequate income levels and an adequate supply of affordable housing. This 'structuralist' perspective has struggled to explain why people experience homelessness for different lengths of time when they face similar conditions in the labour and housing markets. While the supply of affordable housing and access to employment shape people's opportunities to find and secure a home, structural causes do not explain the diversity of people's experiences of homelessness.

Solving the persistent and growing problem of Australian homelessness will take more than identifying the characteristics of the homeless or the causes of homelessness. Only by examining the connections between the causes of homelessness, how people respond to homelessness and how they 'get out' of homelessness can we move social policy towards effective solutions and public perception beyond the attributing of blame.

On the Outside directly focuses on these connections through the stories of people who have experienced homelessness. These voices counter the stereotypical view of the objectified victim that emerges from overly structural accounts, and the pathologised view of homeless people that characterises 'individualistic' (agency) accounts. As Mark Peel notes, it is vital to hear what it is like to be homeless from people who have 'paid the price':

> There are things that being privileged doesn't teach you. From the lowest rung, you see things that aren't visible from the top or the centre. If the shape of a society looks justified, natural and commonsensical to those born or elevated to its leadership, how much more important are the perspectives of those deemed suitable only to be led. The unlucky know more of the world and its vulnerabilities than the lucky; the weak have a far better sense of what matters than the strong. To comprehend the importance of housing or health or employment, listen to the unhoused, the unwell and the unemployed. *(Excerpts from the Homeless Persons Legal Clinic dinner speech by Mark Peel, School of Historical Studies, Monash University, 2006.)*

Perspectives of homeless people enable outsiders to reflect on what is it like to live without the security and stability that people with homes take for granted; to appreciate the crushing burden of being on society's bottom rung; and to gain an insight into the cumulative effects of long-term exclusion from mainstream institutions such as work, family and education and the subsequent loss of self-esteem.

The voices in this book reveal why homelessness affects people in different ways, and also illuminate how different causes relate to different experiences of homelessness and people's strategies for escaping and recovering from homelessness. It is true that people who are homeless encounter a world full of pain, uncertainty and chaos – a world where violence, abuse, social rejection and degradation are common. *On the Outside* shows however, that it is also a world where people form bonds and friendships as a result of their common predicament[3], a world with its own sets of rules and social practices and a world that has its own rhythm, pace and routines. The stories illustrate the way that individuals negotiate the social and material forces that shape the choices available to them and make creative and rational choices to negotiate their situation – one of the toughest experiences in contemporary Australian society.

The people's stories highlight the way that becoming homeless disrupts daily life and how the loss and reinvention of everyday routines shape people's experiences of homelessness. The experience of homelessness is clearly a highly differentiated one, with some people experiencing homelessness for only a short time, some moving in and out of homelessness over many years and some remaining homeless for extended periods of time[4-11]. *On the Outside* argues that the length of time and the impact of homelessness can be better understood by examining people's circumstances before they became homeless, the resources they bring with them and the challenges they face.

In making a link between people's experiences preceding homelessness, their experience of homelessness and how they manage to get out, *On the Outside* emphasises how damaging the experience of homelessness can be. It shows that while some people do avoid the damaging consequences of homelessness, others become deeply mired in the homeless population for many years where their problems often get worse. Many studies have shown that the longer a person is homeless the more likely they will adapt, behaviourally and cognitively, to the contingencies of homelessness – what is commonly termed the acculturation thesis. Some common adaptations include using drugs, involvement and identification with other homeless people, use of welfare agencies and criminal behaviour. These changes, while helpful for survival, make it more difficult for people to get out and stay out of the homeless population[12]. Many of the 'pathologies' commonly linked to the homeless actually emerge as a result of prolonged exposure to homelessness.

What has been overlooked, however, is the way that processes of adaptation are also mediated by the biographical experiences that people bring with them, a distinction that provides the point of departure for this study. A close examination of the relationship between people's biographies, the duration of their homelessness and how they adapt increases understanding of the social processes that result in some people getting stuck in the homeless population, while others, in similar social and economic circumstances, do not.

On the Outside also investigates the issue of cause and consequence. Existing research has established that people who have a short experience of homelessness have different characteristics compared to those who have longer experiences. Among the long-term homeless population there is a disproportionate representation of substance use problems, mental illness, poor physical health and criminal behaviour[13-22]. People with experiences in the state care and child protection system are also over-represented among the long-term homeless population both in Australia and overseas[23-26]. However, there is keen contention amongst researchers about whether these factors are a cause or a consequence of homelessness, which is known as the problem of temporal order[27]. American homelessness researcher Dennis Culhane observes that if disproportionately high rates of these problems are found in the homeless population, that might only mean a high rate for people who get stuck in homelessness[28]. The longitudinal, biographical approach used in *On the Outside* enables clarification of temporal order as well as separation of the processes that lead to homelessness from those that occurred after people become homeless. Distinguishing between characteristics that cause homelessness and those that are a consequence demonstrates how inadequate and one-dimensional the stereotypes of homelessness that circulate in the media and public domain are.

Existing research, both local and international, has ignored the connections between how people become homeless, how long they remain so, what happens to them while they are homeless and how this influences their capacity to *get out* and *stay out* of homelessness. In addressing this gap, *On the Outside* provides a unique insight into the hardships homeless people face and their struggle to surmount them.

In looking at the relationship between becoming homeless, being homeless and exiting homelessness, this study gives service providers and policy makers an evidence-based theory about how different groups of people can resolve their homelessness. We establish which groups are more susceptible to long-term homelessness, and explain how other groups manage to get out relatively quickly. *On the Outside* offers practical suggestions on how to improve responses to homeless people. It suggests that initial assessments of homeless people's needs can be strengthened by focusing some attention on people's biographies and tailoring support and intervention to the pathway that people travel into homelessness on. It also highlights the importance of early intervention, and the provision of permanent housing coupled with ongoing support where it is required. The authors support the broad thrust of the acculturation thesis, which is used by many homelessness researchers, but this book argues that it should be refined to recognise the important influence of people's pasts on their experiences of homelessness. Importantly, *On the Outside* shows that accounts based solely on structure or agency on their own fail to explain the variation in the homeless experience.

As important as these issues are, what the book also reveals is the incredible resilience and determination of homeless people. They are creative and inventive, and they manage to keep on going despite innumerable barriers. The way homeless people cope and survive on the outside of mainstream life is a story that can only be told by the homeless themselves.

APPROACH

Just over 103 homeless households were interviewed as they were leaving emergency accommodation and, after 12 months, 79 of these households were reinterviewed.

The interviews produced rich, detailed and often intimate and highly sensitive information about people's experiences. To protect the confidentiality of the respondents, all identifying information was removed from the transcripts or notes, and then 14 composite cases were produced. This allows the research to quote directly from the powerful statements made by homeless people, while protecting their anonymity.

Much previous research has focused on the demographic characteristics of the homeless population and has attempted to relate these characteristics to different pathways into homelessness. In contrast, this research focuses on the biographical experiences of each person prior to their becoming homeless for the first time. This enables a clearer sense of sequencing and interaction by locating the experience of homelessness in the broader context of an individual's life history.

Secondly, biographical data gives a stronger voice to the lived experience of homelessness. The use of biographical information provides a more dynamic understanding of homelessness and a better answer to the question: why do some people adapt to homelessness, while others, in apparently similar circumstances, do not?

Throughout the book the 'pathways' concept is used to identify some clear patterns within people's unique experiences of homelessness. Along with related metaphors, such as 'homeless careers', the pathways idea has gained increasing research interest as a way to capture the dynamic and differentiated nature of homelessness and other social phenomenon[29-31].

What researchers using the pathways approach have lost sight of, though, is the importance of sequencing different interactions as people travel into, through and out of homelessness. This book uses the pathways approach to distinguish between the paths different groups of people travel into homelessness and to then examine what bearing different pathways into homelessness have on people's experiences of homelessness and their routes out of homelessness.

The research found five typical pathways into homelessness. They are domestic violence, housing crisis, mental health, substance use and people who have their first experience of homelessness before turning 18 years old. It is important to remember that the five pathways are not causal accounts as such, but typifications based on the notion of 'ideal types' developed by the German sociologist Max Weber. 'Ideal types' is an analytical tool that helps to simplify the complicated reality of homelessness in such a way that the connections between the three stages can be seen more clearly.

While the pathways concept provides the framework for this research, concepts such as stigma, routine, the homeless subculture, material and non-material structures are also applied to the analysis. Readers who are interested in a full description of these concepts, along with a definitional framework, can refer to Appendix B.

This book is structured around a three-stage model: the period leading to homelessness, called *becoming* homeless; the lived experience of homelessness, or *being* homeless; and the third stage, which is *exiting* homelessness*. The final chapter discusses the practice and policy implications arising from the research findings.

---

* This three-stage approach closely follows Goffman's schemata for mental patients (1961:122).

BECOMING HOMELESS

1 PATHWAYS INTO HOMELESSNESS

Homelessness is the sum total of our dreams, intentions, errors, omissions, cruelties, kindnesses, all of it recorded, in the flesh, in the life of the streets.

Peter Marin, *Harpers*, Jan 1987

Homeless people become the victims of a collective projection of all that is unpleasant and unsavoury; they come to be the living representatives of parts of everyone that are not accepted ... The repeated look of disgust and fear on the faces of the stranger can provoke and even deepen the feeling that one is disgusting and fearsome/dangerous/violent. This identification with what is projected becomes a great problem for homeless people and is arguably one of the factors that maintains and deepens their problems in general.

John O'Connor, 'Homelessness and the problem of containment', *The European Journal of Psychotherapy, Counselling & Health*, 6 (2) 2003

For some people the shift from housed to homeless happens rapidly, while for others the process is drawn out. Whether it happens quickly or slowly, people's lives are drastically transformed as day-to-day life starts to change, and their routines are disrupted. Individuals manage the disruption to their routines in different ways depending on the nature of their problems and the biographies they bring with them.

Drawing from the experiences of people on each on the five entry pathways we show that individuals negotiate constraints such as housing and employment options, and the shame of becoming homeless in different ways, although there are patterns that occur across each of the five pathways. These patterns have implications for how the process of becoming homeless unfolds, and also for what happens to people while they are homeless.

While no individual fits neatly and completely into a category, the pathway groups show definite patterns in the way the people on each pathway manage the disruption, and how they negotiate the available housing and income limitations.

MENTAL HEALTH PATHWAY

People who experienced mental health problems prior and leading to their first experience of homelessness were the smallest group in the study (6 out of 103). As discussed in chapter 3, they also tend to remain homeless longer than any other group. Three major factors shape the experience of people on this pathway: social attitudes toward mental illness, difficulty meeting labour and housing market demands and the extent of family support.

The negative social attitude, or stigma, attached to mental illness is a profound factor affecting this group. In contemporary society it is not inevitable that mental illness should exclude people from mainstream institutions such as work, housing or the family. We no longer expect that people will be kept out of the way of the community in dedicated psychiatric institutions.

Yet for this group, negative social attitudes towards the mentally ill clearly shaped the nature and extent of their suffering. The stigma of mental illness influenced patterns of interaction with the labour and housing markets and also with other people. Episodes of mental illness, like any health condition, result in a reorganisation of relationships (and interactions) that typically connect people to the broader community. But the stories of this group showed the damaging effects of stigma increased the severity of their problems and contributed to their homelessness.

This group were among the better-educated members of the sample with four of the six completing year 12. Health problems generally emerged in their early 20s and most had their first experience of homelessness a short time after (mean age for the first experience of homelessness is 25 years). As a result, most had maintained independent housing for some time, primarily in private rental. For those who had been evicted, their housing instability could be directly linked to emerging health concerns in a more protracted process of becoming homeless. Similarly, there was evidence of stable work histories for four of the six in this group with employment mainly in blue-collar occupations. The two people who had never worked were also the youngest two members on this pathway. These two people also had little experience in the housing market. Finally, everyone was in receipt of government benefits prior to becoming homeless.

Everyone thought that they had lived 'normal' lives prior to the onset of their mental health problems. While there was a sense that getting by was a struggle for some, they were connected to the mainstream through family and friends, involvement in the housing market and, to a lesser extent, employment.

While the experience of mental health problems is lived in different ways, Tim and Maggie's stories capture the changing patterns of interaction that individuals with mental health issues experience in their move from housed to homeless.

Tim is a 43-year-old single male who has never married. He first became homeless at 32 years of age. Tim is university trained in horticulture, and worked in the field until his late 20s. Tim described his life up to that point as:

> Pretty normal, I mean I wasn't unhappy or anything. I'd been working at the same place for about six years I think.

For most people in this group, the first signs that life was changing were subtle. Tim's problems emerged just prior to his 30th birthday. Tim recalled that he:

> ... had problems remembering things ... when my boss had a go at me, I thought 'stuff him' and had a go back. Then I started to get a bit paranoid.

Maggie is a 26-year-old single woman who lived on her own in a small privately rented flat in the inner city. Maggie commented that her problems:

> ... happened suddenly. I'd been assaulted at a train station. After that I was anxious whenever I went out in public, 'specially at night but I thought it was because of the assault.

Maggie was 19 at the time and not long after had an experience of severe mental illness (known as an 'episode') that scared her 'shitless'. These early episodes signalled the start of more significant changes. Maggie found that she:

> Couldn't sleep at night ... If I couldn't sleep I would play music and this created problems with my neighbours.

Tim had problems with his neighbour's children. When his letterbox was destroyed, he confronted some of the children. They taunted him, calling him 'mad' and 'a nutter'. Tim became agitated and at one stage he:

> ... grabbed hold of one of them. I was shaking with anger and I threw him to the ground. I'd thought I'd hurt him. I'd never been violent before and it shocked me.

As Tim and Maggie tried to make sense of the changes happening in their lives, they also had to grapple with the consequences for their housing and employment options. Both housing and labour markets are highly structured. For example, to maintain a job you must be able to abide by highly formalised and regulated practices such as starting times, required hours and specific job responsibilities. People with mental health issues have to deal with the unpredictable nature of their health problems, making it difficult to comply with the rules that structure the social practices in each market. And for those who were unemployed, complex social security procedures were difficult to negotiate and this could result in problems with income payments.

These difficulties, coupled with the stigma that makes people conceal the source of their problems, leads to destructive consequences and further social exclusion. For instance, Maggie's housing problems started when she:

> ... stopped opening the mail. It just piled up in the corner. The bigger the pile got the worse I felt.

With mounting bills and unpaid rent Maggie's problems got worse. When she stopped answering the phone everything rapidly went downhill:

> It was stupid but I was terrified I would get bad news or something. I buried me head in the sand and got kicked in the arse, that's for sure.

Tim's problems started when his employer issued him with a warning. The warning came 'as a shock' and Tim reacted with a mixture of anger and anxiety:

> I felt betrayed. I'd worked hard and then when things weren't going that well for me he tried to heave me off [sack him].

As existing routines were interrupted and established relationships were reshaped people reported that they felt like they were losing control. The sense of losing control was compounded by the fact that they perceived the source of their problems to be external to them – that is, their problems were caused by other people (employers or the kids next door) or agencies (for example, Centrelink) over whom they had no control.

People on this pathway had to contend with the stigma of 'being mentally ill' both internally and externally. People inevitably internalise broader social attitudes, and the fear associated with mental illness is no exception. For the people in this group, the internalised stigma had a significant role in how they became homeless. For instance, everyone reported that they had feared diagnosis and that their fears were underpinned by an acute concern with being 'given' a stigmatised social identity. In Maggie's words, to be mentally ill was to be a loser, 'a worthless nothing'.

These internalised attitudes made it common for people to deny that they had any mental health problems[1]. Denial is generally a response that mentally ill people employ to reduce public opprobrium. As Tim explained, his behaviour was entirely rational:

> Wouldn't you? You just want to be normal, not branded a loser. I don't have anything against the mentally ill, I just had never thought of myself that way.

Trying to assist people who are in denial of their mental health problems can be complicated. As the following examples show, denial commonly results in people missing out on the material, medical or social assistance that they require.

Although Tim's problems at work stemmed, in part, from his refusal to acknowledge any problems with his mental health, it was only when he received a second warning that the tension in his relationship with his employer triggered an acute episode. Tim said that he:

> ... totally lost the plot. I can't remember the details but I locked myself up at home and didn't move for about two weeks. I just sat there watching telly. I started to think about suicide more and more and cut myself off from the world.

Tim was dismissed soon afterwards. When people's material security is threatened it tends to exacerbate existing health problems and amplify feelings of marginalisation and isolation.

With reduced or insufficient income, both Maggie and Tim faced mounting bills and growing rental arrears. At this point Tim's family became involved. Family support is the third factor that plays a key role in the experiences of this group. Not everyone who has mental health problems has family support but, for those that do, family and friends can provide a buffer that can delay or prevent the situation worsening.

Family support is valuable and also necessarily limited. For example, families struggle when trying to assist a person who does not accept their mental illness. Tim refused to accept his family's assistance as he felt betrayed by them. They said:

> ... I needed help, that I was ill. They tried to trick me into seeing a doctor.

Tim's refusal to acknowledge his problems put a great strain on his family. Furthermore, Tim's suspicion that his family were conspiring against him began to grow when he refused to take his medication:

> They just wanted me to take the medication. I didn't want to. The stuff they give you is awful … anyway I refused and they said take it or you are on your own.

By refusing treatment Tim's health problems got worse and his relationship with his family collapsed.

Maggie's housing problems were compounded because she had few existing supports. Maggie had few friends and no family to assist her or advocate on her behalf. When Maggie's income benefit was reduced for 'missing an appointment or something' her situation reached a critical point. This could have been prevented if she'd had support, but without it Maggie felt like she was:

> … in a washing machine just getting thrown about all over the place. I felt totally fucking lost and unsure. I didn't really know what was happening. I didn't know what to do. I know I felt like giving up.

Nearly 12 months after her first 'episode' the police knocked on her door to inform her that they would be processing the eviction order sometime in the next 24 hours. This was the first Maggie had heard of it. Confronted by homelessness, Maggie overdosed on prescription pills and ended up in hospital 'confused and shocked'. When she was discharged three days later the eviction had proceeded. Now Maggie had no home. Lonely and vulnerable, Maggie had to deal with her homelessness as well as her health problems.

For people who have more substantial social and financial support, the process is more protracted. Six months after losing his job Tim lost his accommodation and was, as he said, 'forced' to accept his family's offer of assistance to move into the family home on a permanent basis. This loss of independence can also contribute to the sense of failure and shame associate with mental illness. In any case, six months later Tim's father died and the family home was sold soon after. His family tried to have him 'committed' and once again he felt angry, abandoned and betrayed. Tim was convinced, 'they wanted me out of the way'.

With less than one week before settlement on the family home, Tim returned to find the place emptied of its contents. This was the 'final straw'. Tim recalled that he:

> Didn't know what to do. I was angry and scared. I'd never been in this position before.

Compounding the problems of this group was a further layer of social isolation shown in their lack of affinity with or empathy towards other people with mental health problems. This behaviour emphasises the destructive effect of a stigmatised identity or experience. While the mentally ill felt marginalised, their attitudes towards other mentally ill people perpetuated the same stereotypes that they actively resisted accepting for themselves. A direct result was that people started to exist in a world where they were neither of the mainstream or belonging to any other group. For most people this marked the beginning of their transition from being a member of the mainstream to being an 'outsider'.

With worsening mental health problems and few, if any, friends or family willing to assist them, individuals on this pathway were forced into boarding houses, caravan parks or onto the streets where they were acutely vulnerable to exploitation. Tim spent his first homeless night huddled up in the laundry of a block of flats:

> . . . not far from dad's place. About five in the morning a torch shining in my eyes woke me up. It was a security guard. A resident had rung and complained. He kicked me out anyway.

For Tim, Maggie and the other people on this pathway into homelessness, life was going to get a lot worse.

DOMESTIC VIOLENCE PATHWAY

The second pathway into homelessness is characterised by physical and sexual violence, psychological abuse and economic deprivation in relationships between adult partners (married or de facto). This is commonly understood as domestic violence[2]. When domestic violence occurs it is usually perpetrated by a man against a woman and it is nearly always women, often accompanied by children, who leave home[3-5].

There are three key factors generally encountered by people on this pathway: violence, the stigma associated with domestic violence, and low income due to women's poorer labour market opportunities.

There were 14 people in this group. These people were predominantly women and became homeless at a later age than people on the other pathways. Of the 14 cases, 12 were families and these households had 26 children under the age of 18 with a mean age of 8 years. The remaining two households were recorded as single person households, although in both cases children had been removed by state authorities or were in the care of other family members. These two women saw themselves as doubly stigmatised – they had been forced out of their homes and also believed that they were viewed as irresponsible parents, as 'bad mothers' incapable of taking care of their children.

Prior to the onset of violence, life had been about work and raising a family. Most had left school early with 80 per cent leaving before or at the end of year 10. Everyone had worked at some point in their lives, although for most working was about earning additional income to help make ends meet, rather than a distinct career of their own. For eight of the women there was some degree of housing instability prior to becoming homeless. Each of these households reported that they had previously been evicted, some more than once, although these problems with their housing were typically due to affordability issues rather than domestic violence.

While there was variation in the experience of domestic violence, Lyn and Sandra are representative of the women in this category. Both women were in their 30s and had children. Neither Sandra nor Lyn had paid employment at the time they became homeless, although Sandra was a qualified hairdresser. Lyn had been with her partner for seven years and lived in suburban Melbourne. Sandra had been married for 10 years and lived in country Victoria.

Prior to experiencing domestic violence many women reported periods of relative stability in their family life. Lyn recounted that for the first two years of her marriage:

> ... everything was OK. We had some arguments and we struggled a bit, but John was working and we'd started to think about buying a home.

Domestic stability was reflected in the predictability of day-to-day life. Lyn and Sandra's aspirations were modest, and focussed on work, family and home. Their experiences highlight the notion that 'home' is not merely a physical space, but a 'site of constancy in the social and material environment', a place 'in which the day-to-day routines of human existence are performed ... a base around which identities are constructed'[6]. For Lyn, domestic stability began to change when her partner was retrenched and struggled to find a new job:

> He did bits and pieces for about six months or so, but he was getting disillusioned and quite depressed. He started to drink more ... he became abusive.

The onset of domestic violence changes patterns of interaction in family life. Relationships based on affection and cooperation are transformed into relationships based on fear and coercion. Past relationships that provided security, continuity and predictability are removed. Domestic violence reorganises relationships between family members.

In most cases physical violence was preceded by verbal and psychological abuse. This steadily eroded any form of security and constancy in the lives of these women and their children. Over a 12-month period Lyn noted that John's behaviour became increasingly erratic and the family tried to avoid him when he was drunk:

> … the kids were terrified of him and would try to steer clear of him. Jade would stay in her room for hours.

As the verbal abuse became more frequent it signalled the onset of physical violence. When Lyn complained that she did not have enough money for food and that his drinking was a problem, John physically assaulted her for the first time. Lyn realised that her world had now changed, but she:

> … didn't know what to do. I was terrified, he had never touched me before. He had turned into a monster. I cried for days.

Women spoke about becoming prisoners in their own homes once physical violence was introduced to the relationship. The breakdown of normal patterns of interaction within the family turned 'home' into a site of domination and powerlessness. In Sandra's case her partner started to treat her:

> ... like a fucking slave. I was his cook and his cleaner.

Women tried to resist the physical and emotional domination, but fear of retribution and a lack of alternatives shaped their reactions. Lyn:

> ... desperately wanted to talk to someone but I was so afraid John would find out and take it out on me and the kids.

For others the situation became more extreme. After one violent assault left her with a broken nose and two black eyes, Sandra remembered the:

> ... look on the nurse's face when I told her I'd tripped ... she knew I was lying.

Covering up the perpetrator's behaviour was a common practice. When Sandra returned home from the hospital her partner:

> Didn't give a flying fuck about me ... he was only interested in what I'd told the hospital staff. He threatened to kill me if I told anyone.

While fear prevented many women from seeking assistance, an acute sense of shame and embarrassment contributed as well. Lyn tried to conceal the problem from her friends and neighbours:

> I didn't want them to know what was happening. I tried to pretend
> it was all OK.

In these early stages, people commonly refused to accept that violence had begun to dominate their lives.

This denial stems in part from the perceived negative reflection of domestic violence on the social and self-identity of the victims. This draws attention to the second factor relevant to this group – the stigma attached to domestic violence. Women who are the victims of violence also have to deal with the stigma of being in violent households, showing that these experiences occur in 'gendered terrain in which women's housing needs and experiences remain marginalised'[7].

For Sandra and others, their response was to try and maintain the appearance of normality:

> All my friends thought we were a good couple, well at the start they
> did anyway. I tried to make everything look better than it was I
> suppose.

Ultimately, however, attempts to conceal problems were in vain. Hiding family violence is difficult because the physical signs such as bruising do not go unnoticed. The noise of violent quarrels and children screaming meant that people soon suspected 'things weren't going OK'. Lyn assumed that her neighbours and friends 'knew we had problems but we all tried to pretend things were OK'. These feelings were particularly strong for women living in rural areas. Cibich[8] argues that this occurs because rural communities are often tight-knit and geographical isolation makes hiding the situation even more difficult. Sandra's situation reflected this:

> It was obvious people knew. No one dropped in anymore and on the street people would avoid me or have to be somewhere else when they saw me.

Women's attempts to conceal the problem often reflected their shame and fears. A key fear was that authorities would remove children from their care. Sandra's sister had 'lost' her children and the thought of losing her children:

> … terrified me. I wanted to be seen as a good mother. I didn't want people to think I couldn't raise my kids.

The second concern centred on the disruption to their children's schooling and their after-school routines. These concerns emphasise the importance of a stable environment for children, as well as drawing out broader issues connected to their social identities as mothers. Lyn reported that she:

> Didn't want the other parents to find out … to think I was a bad mother.

Women experiencing domestic violence have to deal with the stigma of being battered and, for those with children, the stigma of being 'unworthy mothers' as well.

As their relationships became more unpredictable and the violence more common, self-esteem and confidence began to diminish. Many felt they had contributed in some way to the problem and consequently that they had failed their children. Lynn felt that she had 'betrayed the kids. I felt I was a lousy mum.'

For women involved in domestic violence, the loss of control and the negative social stigma resulted in the abandonment of many of their social networks[9]. These changing patterns of social interaction increase the vulnerability of women in violent relationships, which in turn increases their susceptibility to homelessness. In this context the question is often asked why women experiencing domestic violence stay when it is clear that their family is 'falling apart'.

Lyn threatened to walk out on John but she didn't know where to go or who could help. In addition, many wanted to believe that the situation could change and return to normal. Deep down Lyn hoped that:

> John could and would change. All we needed was a bit of luck for John to get a job. I didn't want to accept that our relationship was in bad shape.

Making a decision to leave was made harder by repeated promises of change and convincing expressions of remorse. Lyn said that on numerous occasions:

> John promised to change … he begged us to forgive him and we did, time and time again. It was hard not to with the kids and all that.

While deep emotional connections mediated Lyn's responses, the thought of leaving started to dominate her thoughts more and more:

> I wanted out. I wanted to take the kids and find somewhere peaceful and quiet. I felt paralysed ... I couldn't seem to figure out what to do.

When families are in turmoil and relationships between adult family members sour, issues of stigma and shame, combined with escalating tension and violence, pull women in different directions.

Some women in this study withdrew and some ran, while others tried to pretend that there were no problems at home.

The third factor influencing the behaviour of these women was a lack of economic resources. While violence against women cuts across all social classes, service providers indicate that those women who become homeless tend to be 'drawn from poorer economic backgrounds'[10].

After another violent episode, Sandra was desperate to escape. Sandra took her children and stayed with her mother but after two weeks they:

> ... couldn't stay at mum's any longer, and I was too embarrassed to ask our friends. I tried to get private rental but could not find anything that I could afford. I went home and the abuse soon started again.

Often the decision to return 'home' was made because few women had independent financial resources and most had left all of their possessions behind. Sandra had 'walked out' on four or five occasions over a space of twelve months. In each instance she returned home because she could not find affordable accommodation and she continued to believe that things would get better.

The cycle of violence in abusive relationships has been well documented with studies suggesting that anywhere between one-third and one-half of those women who leave, return to abusive situations[11-15].

While there was variation in the intensity, frequency and duration of violence, the dominant pattern in these 14 cases was 'in and out' behaviour. For many this had occurred over a number of years. In the early stages, many women wanted to reconcile with their partners. These women had invested in the relationship and wanted the relationship to continue as long as the violence stopped. However for most the problems did not stop and Lyn eventually recognised that she had to:

> ... get out of there forever. It was getting worse. He had promised to change but didn't.

Not only did a lack of economic independence make leaving difficult, but each time Sandra left her partner tracked her down and she returned home, lured by the promise of change. But after:

> ... he hit Josh (their three-year-old son) we left. I'd had enough. We weren't coming back.

Physical violence directed at children commonly signals an end to the relationship.

Not only did these women have to come to terms with being victims of domestic violence, the collapse of their relationships and the breakdown in their routines, they now had to deal with the prospect of being homeless. This was a prospect that 'terrified' them almost as much as the violence at home.

HOUSING CRISIS PATHWAY

For 24 households, a series of financial crises precipitated their entry into the homeless population. These crises took many forms but their cumulative impact stretched the financial capacity of these households to breaking point. Their low level of financial resources meant that events others in the community could absorb pushed these households into a financial spiral that ended in eviction and, ultimately, homelessness.

While housing and labour market conditions affect everyone who becomes homeless, they were the primary factors shaping the experience of this group*. In particular, there were three typical ways through which housing crisis came about: job loss, sustained poverty, and the gentrification of inner city housing markets.

The group on the housing crisis pathway had the most diverse characteristics. Overall, families accounted for 58 per cent, with sole parent families accounting for a significant majority of these (79 per cent). Most people experienced homelessness for

---

* The housing crisis pathway is modelled on the ideas outlined by Chamberlain and Johnson (2002), Wasson and Hill (1998), Timmer, Eitzen and Talley (1994) and Mulroy and Lane (1992).

the first time in their early 30s (mean age 31), although the age people first experienced homelessness varied considerably, with ages ranging from 19 to 50. Many people had been employed in the past, although by the time of the research everyone's sole source of income was government benefits. Most had been on government benefits for some time (mean duration 16 months). There were few reported problems with drugs or alcohol, no reported problems with violence and there were no reports of mental health problems preceding homelessness.

Frank, Sally, Lee and John are representative of the people who experienced a housing crisis and became homeless. Frank was a trained butcher who, because of a workplace injury nearly a decade ago, was on a disability pension. Frank was 47 years old and single because his partner had died soon after his accident. He had no children and lived, long term, in a small flat in the inner city. Frank was a heavy smoker and by his own admission was in poor health.

Lee and John were high school sweethearts and were married soon after they left school. Lee (32) and John (36) had three children – two in primary school and one in year 8. Prior to their homelessness Lee and John rented privately in the south-eastern suburbs of Melbourne.

Sally was a 29-year-old single mother with three-year-old twins. The father of the twins left her six months after their birth and Sally had raised the children on her own for two-and-a-half years. Sally had also lived in private rental, although she had never been in paid employment.

Prior to their becoming homeless 13 of the 24 households had stable housing over a number of years. This was particularly apparent among dual parent families where it was common to find at least one person with a relatively stable work history. Housing stability was reflected in the predictability of day-to-day life and it was common to see life structured around the constraints of 'normality' – family, school and work. Lee and John's lives:

> … revolved around the kids. Taking them to school, out to their friends', making the kids' lunches, doing laundry. Just normal stuff, nothing fancy.

Stable housing provided constancy, a sense of control and a secure base where family life and day-to-day routines were nurtured. There were stresses however. Neil and Fopp[16] point out that it is common for people in poverty to experience intermittent financial crisis. This was the case for nearly half of this group as the effects of poverty sporadically disrupted their lives. There was substantial evidence that eleven people had experienced recurring housing problems over many years and it was common to see housing careers punctuated by evictions and the loss of accommodation. Sally had been:

> … in three or four places in the last seven years or so. Every time I'd get settled something would happen – one time the place was sold and at the next the owner wanted his sister to have the place.

This pre-homeless pattern of residential instability reminds us that some people are vulnerable to homelessness simply because of their low income.

A poor financial position was the dominant reason these households became homeless. This vulnerability manifested itself in a number of different ways. In many cases the source of their financial problems emanated from outside the housing system. In these cases the event that precipitated homelessness could generally be traced to the loss of a job. This was the case with Lee and John.

Since leaving school John had always worked and for the last six years he had been with the same company. When the company folded John's initial reaction was that:

> It'd sort itself out. I didn't expect any problems finding something. I wasn't that choosy.

After four months John still hadn't found a job and, given that John and Lee's housing had been geared to a working income, they soon began to struggle financially. Lee said the family had:

> Never been late with the rent but now we were struggling to pay our bills. We owed nearly $900 in back rent.

After seven months John had only done a bit of part-time work and the family's problems were becoming acute:

> We got behind in the rent. We'd cut back on so many things, but Edward needed school books and the kids needed uniforms. We had to borrow money from John's parents.

As the financial pressures became more acute many households were forced to reduce household expenses. However, in already tight household budgets there was little scope for saving and, as a way of reducing costs, many households looked for cheaper accommodation. After 12 months John still had no work. When the family received a threatening letter from the landlord they decided to look for a cheaper place. They found a cheaper property, but the costs of moving put them under greater financial pressure:

> We didn't think it through and it cost us more than we expected –
> there were all these costs connecting the phone and the electricity
> … we did most of the moving ourselves but it still cost a couple of
> hundred bucks for the truck.

Whatever financial reserves these households had, and low-income households seldom have much[17], were eroded by the cost of moving house. What made the situation worse for families was that moving invariably disrupted the children's schooling and took the family away from the community where they had established social connections. As the Human Rights and Equal Opportunity Commission[18] noted, acute residential instability (as opposed to frequent moving by choice or design) impacts on the emotional and psychological resources of every household member. This was clearly evident in this group.

With their normal routines in disarray, and accumulating financial problems, arguments became 'more common' as the emotional reserves of the family were stretched. Lee felt like:

… everything was slipping away. A lot of things came up at once –
bills, school, Edward's teeth – and we found it harder and harder
to cope.

Sally's case highlights the impact of sustained poverty on
people's housing stability and on their sense of connectedness
and belonging. Sally lost contact with many of her friends
because of her frequent moves over the years:

I haven't seen anyone for months. I used to be more social but sort
of drifted away from my friends. What with twins and living out
here it's, well, lonely.

Sally's record of previous evictions reduced her rental options and
forced her to look for accommodation in areas where she had no
history or connections:

The only reason we're out here is that I could afford a place. Before
we moved out here I didn't even know the place existed to tell you
the truth.

Away from her local area, Sally couldn't access vital social
supports, like childcare help from family, neighbours or friends.
Without access to this sort of social capital, Sally faced her
problems alone. Sally's housing had always been 'a struggle' and
now with twins her expenses just seemed to grow:

They were sick all the time, nothing major just gripes and that. It
was always both of them too.

Sally gradually sank into debt. She owed about $400 to the local chemist, had outstanding gas and electricity bills and she owed money to her sister as well:

> You look around the house, see the food getting low, bills due here, bills due there, it's hard to know what to do.

When Sally responded to the chemist's demand that she pay the outstanding amount, it meant:

> I couldn't pay the rent on time. John [the landlord] was alright about it, but I could tell he wasn't happy.

No matter what Sally did she lived in a state of perpetual financial crisis and this meant that any routines she established were constantly disrupted, creating further anxiety.

Studies of homelessness frequently make the point that single parent families on low incomes are vulnerable to homelessness and it does not take much to push them into crisis[19].

Sally's flat was cold and draughty and with sick twins she ran a small heater for most of the day during winter. When the first bill arrived:

> It was massive. There was definitely something dodgy about the electricity and I complained … it didn't do anything though; I still had an electricity bill that I couldn't afford.

When problems emerge for households in poverty, bills mount and debts accumulate and people often have to make a decision about which bills to pay. While people react in different ways the consequences are similar.

Sally had to make a decision whether to pay the rent or have the electricity cut off. Sally paid the electricity bill and this time her landlord was less sympathetic when her rent was overdue:

> He sent a notice … it was pretty clear – pay up or get out. I couldn't afford the rent and I couldn't afford to leave.

Similarly, Lee and John remained in financial crisis and while they focused on maintaining their new housing, this came at a price:

> We'd slipped into arrears again so we didn't pay the phone bill and the phone was cut off. It wasn't so much the phone being cut off that worried us, it was that our daughter went nuts … she was embarrassed … everyone has a phone.

Three decades ago the Henderson Poverty Inquiry noted that the:

> … effects of a very low income mean that families are placed under constant stress which makes the family members particularly vulnerable … Second, when trouble does occur, the effects are likely to be far reaching for the low income family which has fewer resources to resolve it[20].

The gentrification of inner city housing markets was the third way a housing crisis manifested itself. In the inner city the impact of gentrification has contributed to increasing land values and rents, and people on fixed low incomes are particularly vulnerable to being squeezed out of the housing market[21].

This was Frank's experience. Frank had been a tenant in the same flat for over a decade. As Frank's health worsened he found it difficult to make ends meet. Nevertheless he would:

> ... manage somehow. I always paid my bills, maybe a bit late sometimes, but I always paid my bills.

The block of flats Frank lived in was going to be redeveloped and when he received a 90-day Notice To Vacate (NTV) he was initially:

> Annoyed more than anything else. I'd grown used to my place and knew lots of people. I didn't want to move.

When he started to look for another place he was:

> Shocked ... I looked around but couldn't find anything cheap enough. I was paying $120 a week and there was nothing under $160. It may not sound like much, but $40, where was I supposed to get that?

People on low incomes who are affected by gentrification generally have few housing options. Frank contacted the Office of Housing with less than a month to go before he was supposed to move out but they told him:

> They couldn't do anything until I was homeless. What use is that? They have it the wrong way around.

Frank became increasingly anxious. When he was 'knocked back for the umpteenth time' on a flat he 'couldn't really afford', Frank faced the prospect of becoming homeless. In his late 40s, in poor health and a long-term inner city resident, Frank was unsure what to do. Frank's tenancy was extended for a month but after that he was forced out and he moved in with his sister on a temporary basis. His sister lived:

> ... on the other side of the city. I didn't know anyone, it was cramped and I had a flat full of furniture to store.

Whether people's problems are related to the housing market or to insufficient income, or a combination of both, these processes can unfold at different rates.

Some people moved from being housed to homeless in a short space of time, but for most it took much longer. Most fought to maintain their housing using a variety of strategies such as borrowing money from family and friends, cutting costs, using credit cards, moving, leaving bills unpaid, selling household goods and, occasionally, crime. While the strategies varied by age and household type, they all emphasise the resilience and resourcefulness of these people. However, without additional income, cheaper housing or family support these strategies simply delayed the inevitable.

It is important to make the point that for most households it took more than a single crisis to precipitate homelessness. What separates these households from other similarly economically vulnerable households is that they were eventually overwhelmed by a series of problems, a 'run of bad luck' or a sustained 'reversal of fortunes' as Rossi[22] puts it. While the final event or issue may appear innocuous (a heating bill for instance), it is the compounding effects of ongoing financial problems that steadily strips away their financial resources, which defines the experiences of these 24 people.

With debts accumulating and with no access to additional resources, all it took was an additional setback to precipitate the first episode of homelessness. Sally had been driving an unregistered car and when the:

> ... cops pulled me up they put a canary [unroadworthy certificate] on the car. They told me I had some outstanding fines. I'd already borrowed money and owed heaps. My credit card was maxed out [at its limit]. I mean I had no options.

No matter what the final catalyst, everyone's housing situation reached a critical point – with nowhere to go and eviction imminent, a significant minority (42 per cent) abandoned their property. Sally knew that she:

> ... was going to get evicted anyway and I was already on the landlord black list as well* and I had no chance of getting into public housing.

Sally had accepted that she was going to be evicted and she had started to make alternative, albeit temporary, arrangements:

---

* To screen prospective tenants real estate agents increasingly rely on Residential Tenancy Databases (RTDs). These databases maintain information on tenants to assist property managers to 'assess risk and identify potential problems'.

A mate said she would put me and the kids up in her flat for a month or so. Knowing that I did a runner.

Sally and her twins spent the night on the lounge room floor in a single bedroom flat. While Sally 'did a runner' the majority (58 per cent) of the group were 'formally' evicted. For Lee and John the day the eviction order was served:

Will stay with us forever. We woke up and knew we had nowhere to go. Everything was in boxes … I can honestly say I had never felt so despairing … John was shell shocked.

That night Lee, John and their children had their first experience of homelessness. It would leave a lasting impression on them all.

SUBSTANCE USE PATHWAY

In contrast to popular understandings, problematic substance use was the entry to homelessness for only 17 per cent of the people in the study. Though, as we shall discuss later, 55 per cent of people reported substance use issues with many problems emerging as a result of their experiences of homelessness. Two inter-related factors influenced the experience of becoming homeless for this group: negative community attitudes towards illicit drug use and the requirements of the labour market.

John, a 26-year-old single male, originally from Perth, was one of 18 adults in the sample whose involvement with drugs was the dominant factor that led to their homelessness. He left school when he was 16, travelling and working around Australia until he was 20 years old. He settled in Melbourne doing intermittent work with a printing firm as well as occasionally working on the production line at a tobacco factory. John also had a heroin problem but says that 'no one sets out to become a junkie'. John's experiences illustrate that most people on this pathway had relatively normal lives prior to developing a drug dependency.

Five of these respondents also reported alcohol problems. However, four of these respondents said their alcohol problems emerged after an ongoing drug problem. Along with John, the experiences of Michelle and Keith are representative of people whose problematic substance use led to homelessness. Michelle was a 39-year-old graphic artist whose life had been 'somewhat bohemian'. Michelle and her partner had been together, on and off, for 10 years and they had lived together for most of that time in the inner city. By the time she was 30 Michelle had a successful career and a heroin habit.

Michelle went to a private school and both her parents were professionals. This example highlights one distinctive feature of this pathway. In the sample of 103, there were 83 cases where the family's occupational background could be established and the overwhelming majority (90 per cent) were from blue-collar families. In contrast 29 per cent of dependent drug users reported that they grew up in white-collar families. This is important because people from higher socioeconomic backgrounds typically have access to more resources. It is these resources that can prevent homelessness. However, what these cases show is that the resources of the middle class are finite, and while they can prolong the pre-homeless phase, ultimately, when substance use 'controls the day', they cannot prevent it.

Keith (27) was a single male who was a qualified plumber. By the time he was 24 Keith had been working for a major plumbing company for eight years and had been living in the same flat for four years. He also had a problem with heroin.

John, Michelle and Keith all had stable, independent accommodation histories prior to becoming homeless. In most cases people were in their late teens when they were introduced to drugs by their friends. Keith was about 19 when his friend suggested that he give 'harry' [heroin] a go:

> I hadn't been tempted before but it didn't seem to be doing Terry any harm. We went into the bathroom. I'd never injected anything so Terry did it for me. I was crook for a while, but after that it was grouse.

Michelle was about 23 when she was introduced to heroin through her best friend's boyfriend:

> I'd been around there dozens of times with her, but wasn't really interested. One night he offered some. I was hesitant but Tess had a go, so I thought, why not? I was just curious.

In the same way that not everyone who drinks becomes an alcoholic, many people experiment with heroin but not everyone becomes drug dependent. Surveys of heroin users here and overseas suggest that the ratio of occasional users to frequent users is around 8:1[23].

The group of users interviewed for this research started as occasional users, but as they overcame their initial fears they progressed from occasional to more frequent use. Keith says that he:

> ... was scoring every week or so, but I could go without it. There were a few of us who were using and we all worked ... it didn't seem like an issue at the time. I'd only do it on the weekends.

Apart from the pattern of stable accommodation, there was also evidence of stable work histories. In fact, many people spoke of how they managed to maintain a 'casual habit' for many years before they became homeless. These people worked and held onto their accommodation while using drugs like heroin or speed. Michelle said that she and her partner:

> Had been using for about five or six years before we had any real problems. I'd worked the whole time and no one apart from a few close friends knew that I did it. It was sort of a secret.

While the illegal nature of drug use provided a basis for keeping it a secret, most people were keen to avoid being associated with heroin, or labelled a 'junkie' – a strongly stigmatised social identity even among users[24]. This demonstrates a strong recognition among users of the negative community attitudes towards illicit substance use. Keith said that he 'wasn't a junkie or anything like that ... I could take it or leave it'. For Keith, having a job distinguished him from the junkies. Work enabled him to maintain his accommodation and at the same time to continue casual use. At this stage Keith's substance use could be incorporated into his daily routines without drastically altering them.

For the 10 people who had jobs when they started using heroin, the process of becoming homeless typically extended over a number of years. In contrast, those people who were on government benefits tended to slip into crisis more rapidly. Over time, however, the pattern that emerged for both the employed and unemployed was that casual use escalated to the point where drugs dominated daily life. This marks a significant point in their drug career. By the time he was 24 Keith had:

> ... been using on and off for about four years, maybe a bit less, but a fair time anyhow. Anyway I'd started to use a lot more frequently.

As drug use escalated it soon became problematic because it consumed a majority of available income and 'shaped the day'[25]. When drugs dominate day-to-day life, routines that link people to a range of social and economic structures cannot be maintained. As life became increasingly chaotic and focused on 'scoring' the first major material change emerged. For those who were working, their drug dependency made it increasingly difficult to maintain normal work routines.

Similar to those struggling with mental health problems, people in this group found it impossible to meet the highly structured requirements of the labour market. The unpredictability of using and scoring creates different and ultimately unsustainable patterns of interaction with the labour market. Exclusion from the labour market is common among homeless people, but the way individual actors engage in or respond to this process varies according to individual biographies and the issues that people bring with them. Michelle's drug use became problematic when she:

> ... started to miss work. When I was there my work was getting pretty sloppy. I tried to keep it together.

After four years of casual use Keith was now scoring:

> Four, five times a week maybe, maybe more. Anyways, I'd fuck off from work sometimes and my boss and I started to have a few problems.

Two days before his 25th birthday the company let Keith go. Without work both Keith and Michelle were in the same financial position as John, and it did not take long before they all had problems with their accommodation. John, who was on government benefits, said he could not:

> ... pay the rent. I thought I could get on top of it, but it didn't work out that way ... I starting to get involved in a bit of dealing, a few burgs [burglaries] and that sort of thing to keep me going but it just sorta got out of control.

Over time 'traditional' routines broke down and many social relationships disintegrated as people looked for ways to 'fund their habit'. For Michelle this included:

> Stealing stuff from my parents' place … all sorts of stuff – cash, jewellery, even booze and pills. They caught me red-handed. It broke them up real bad.

Michelle's drug use moved from a private activity, limited to a small circle of close friends, into her family's world. This exposure was a shaming experience and led her to withdraw further into the drug-using scene. With her relationship to her family broken and few pre-homeless friendships remaining, Michelle's social networks comprised almost entirely of other users. In this context the very behaviour that was the source of their problems was normalised. For Michelle, using dominated all of her social interactions. Similarly, using heroin consumed all of Keith's economic resources and when he found himself in massive arrears he decided to:

> … move in with three other blokes into a flat … I knew it was a shooting gallery. All I did every day seemed to revolve around drugs – scoring and using.

Some people resorted to stealing, while others sold their personal belongings to fund their habit. Over a four-month period Keith sold all his plumbing equipment. Not only did this limit Keith's work options, he sold his gear for:

... peanuts. I was so desperate I sold tools worth thousands of dollars for nics [nothing].

Michelle and her partner tried to hold onto their accommodation but they had:

Already sold everything ... we were living a hand-to-mouth existence.

If drug use becomes problematic, people are usually caught between maintaining their accommodation and maintaining an expensive habit.

For this group the habit won. Two days before John and his flatmates were due to be evicted for 'massive arrears' John left:

I didn't have any money but I knew a squat where a few people were staying, so I headed down there. It was a pretty ordinary scene down there ... fits everywhere, shit all over the place.

Keith and Michelle also lost their accommodation. Michelle found it:

... hard to believe how far down we had fallen. We had hit rock bottom. I was too embarrassed to try and get any help so we spent the night on the beach.

By the time this group entered the homeless population, their interactions with the labour and housing markets and their nonusing peers were distorted, and they were already immersed in a using subculture. Keith slept on a filthy couch in a property being used by an 'ex'-junkie, but Keith's only concern was 'getting some gear; everything else, even housing, was secondary'. For all of them, their routines would be shaped by the need to raise money and the consuming nature of their drug dependency. Both aspects would combine to compromise their ability to get out and stay out of the homeless population.

YOUTH PATHWAY

The final entry pathway is the largest, with 41 people reporting that they had their first experience of homelessness before they were 18. Prior to the 1980s youth homelessness was not a major social issue. This changed, however, in the 1980s when advocates and service providers noticed that increasing numbers of young people were seeking assistance. This prompted significant service system reform in 1985[26]. However, it was not until 1989, with the release of the Human Rights and Equal Opportunities Commission (HREOC) report *Our Homeless Children* (1989), that youth homelessness emerged as a significant public issue in Australia.

Researchers have identified a range of factors that mediate young people's entry into the homeless population – issues relating to family type, sexual preference, mental health status and ethnicity are commonly cited triggers. Local research findings frequently cite family conflict as a 'cause' of youth homelessness[27-30]. The Burdekin Report noted that family conflict 'features strongly in most studies of young people leaving home' (1989:88). The National Committee for the Evaluation of Youth Services Support Scheme[31] found that 78 per cent of young people had experienced some form of conflict prior to leaving home, with the rate increasing to over 85 per cent for those who left home before they were 16. In his study of 100 homeless young people, O'Connor[32] expressed indirect agreement when he reported that 'family conflict is the unifying theme in all of the accounts'. In our sample there was variation in the way young people left home, but family problems were always the underlying issue.

Conflict at home can vary in extent, frequency and duration. Family conflict has been used to describe a range of issues from arguments between siblings to sexual abuse. While conflict may lead to homelessness, conflict can also be a symptom of deeper problems such as abuse or neglect. Framed in this way, family conflict is a broad and difficult concept to measure. However, O'Connor[33] argues that considering family conflict as the root cause of homelessness is incorrect when there is abuse or neglect present. Similarly, Hutson and Liddiard's (1994) study of youth homelessness in London makes an explicit distinction between family conflict and physical and sexual abuse when they make the point that 'family conflict can be instrumental in forcing a young person to leave as can physical or sexual abuse.' This emphasises the importance of distinguishing between family conflict and physical or sexual abuse – both are significant, but they are also very different.

In this section we make a distinction between young people whose family conflict was underpinned by normative resistance to parental controls and restrictions, whom we term 'dissenters', and those where 'family conflict' was underpinned by physical or sexual abuse or involvement in the state care and protection system, whom we term 'escapers'. Of the 41 people on this pathway, there were 32 escapers. Most of the 32 (94 per cent) had histories of institutional, foster or residential care. All of them had backgrounds characterised by high residential mobility, little familial or social stability and most had experienced abusive family relations over many years. Home, for this group, was not associated with security and safety, but was linked to violence, material and psychological deprivation and ongoing disruption. For most, family relations were dysfunctional and in many cases their families had simply disintegrated around them. As Crane and Brannock[34] note, for many homeless young people, home effectively leaves them. Robbie, Toni and Andrew's experiences were representative of the escapers.

This left a small group of nine dissenters. For these people their responses to what they perceived to be excessive parental control had created tension within their family and this had escalated to the point where a return home was unlikely, if not impossible.

Although less than one-quarter of those on the youth pathway were classified as dissenters this should not be interpreted as meaning that they are a minority in the youth homeless population. There is strong evidence to suggest that the number of dissenters would be considerably larger in a sample drawn from different sources[35, 36]. Although correctly quantifying the two groups is important, the core processes underlying the lived experiences of both groups – how they respond to the stigma of homelessness and how they interact with the homeless subculture – can still be analysed even though the escapers are likely to be over-represented.

Dissenters

The nine dissenters were all living with their families prior to their becoming homeless. The primary issue that dissenters had to contend with was family values and rules. While family values and household rules vary from house to house, it is the rejection of the normatively prescribed rules that are at the heart of this group's problems.

Although there is variation among the dissenters, Nan's experiences leading to homelessness were typical. Nan is sixteen, single and still at school. Nan's family came from Vietnam when she was three. When she was eleven her mother died and three years later her father remarried. Nan clashed with her stepmother and around the time she was 15 she started to spend nights at her friends' places without her parents' permission.

Nan's case illustrates two issues commonly reported among young homeless people. First, for second generation young Australians, problems at home sometimes occur as a result of a tension between the parents' traditional values and the values young people develop at school. Nan's father did not like her staying out without permission, or going out on weeknights. According to Nan he was 'very strict compared to my friends' parents.'

In some cases it is the young person's emerging identity that conflicts with the 'traditional family values'[37]. In other cases problems occur as a result of young people directly questioning and challenging the authority of their parents, and rebelling against what they perceive as excessive parental control.

This was emphasised in cases where parents tried to restrict or control the son or daughter's choice of partner. These cases were a minority, but in each case there was what Chamberlain and Mackenzie describe as 'in and out' behaviour. This is where young people would stay out for a few nights and then return home for a period of time before repeating the pattern. Eventually Nan was given an ultimatum – accept her parents' authority or leave. Nan left.

Often young people like Nan are blamed for leaving home – Nan could have accepted her parents' authority, but by rejecting their rules and values Nan 'chose' to be homeless. Placing the blame directly onto young people is evident in public discussion, which frequently relies on the issue of choice to explain youth homelessness. This attitude is best captured in a newspaper article that appeared soon after the Burdekin Report was released in 1989. In the article the *Sydney Morning Herald* proclaimed that:

> In the eastern suburbs a vast majority have homes to go to ... the children choose to live on the streets[38].

The use of choice to explain why so many young people experience homelessness is important because the notion of choice invokes a particular morality in which the young person, irrespective of the context in which they leave home, 'must accept responsibility for any difficulties they subsequently encounter'[39]. When choice is used to explain youth homelessness it implicitly supports the view that young homeless people do not deserve any assistance. Certainly, there are some young people who are attracted by the excitement of the streets, but Nan's problems at home, like the other dissenters, were sustained and serious. For the dissenters life at home had become unbearable and their decision to leave home was made in the context of deeply fractured family relationships. Often when choice is used to explain youth homelessness these contextual factors are ignored. Hirst[40] wrote of the young people she interviewed:

> These young people rarely choose to leave a comfortable home or a stable life for life on the streets or the refuge roundabout. If they had left as a matter of free choice just to further their experience they would have soon returned home.

Clearly, to make sense of the reasons why young people leave home requires a better explanation than that they choose to leave.

Escapers

The experiences of escapers preceding homelessness was different from that of the dissenters. This occurs because the escapers had to deal with three different structures. The first is dealing with physical or psychological abuse, or 'adverse childhood experiences'. The second structural factor involves dealing with the stigma of coming from a dysfunctional family. The third structural factor that escapers have to contend with is their poor position in the labour market. It is how these factors interact, and how they are mediated through individual biographies, that produces the distinct career trajectory of the escapers.

Toni, Andrew and Robbie's experiences are typical of this group. Toni is 17 and she has a two-year-old daughter who is currently in foster care. Toni's parents were both under 18 when she was born and they split up by the time she was seven. Toni lived with her mother in the western suburbs of Melbourne and her mother had a mental health problem as well as an addiction to prescription pills. As a result, Toni was in and out of foster care from the time she was eight until she was 13. She has two sisters and a brother (all younger) who are in a similar position. From the time Toni was nine she had to deal with the unpredictable behaviour of her mother. Occasionally her mum would:

> Forget about us. She'd disappear for a few days on end and then come home with someone. I learnt to be pretty independent from early on.

Toni and the rest of the family had to deal with their mother's erratic behaviour as well as temporary additions to the household. As the eldest, Toni found it particularly hard when her mother would:

> Come home with these creeps. They'd try and boss me around, you know be the dad, all full of authority and shit.

There was strong evidence among all the escapers of sustained housing instability prior to becoming homeless. Toni was always being:

> ... moved from one place to another. I'd stay with mum for a while then things would get too much and I'd be fostered out for a while. Then back to mum's ... it went on like that for years.

Not only was there little domestic stability in their lives, for many, home was a site of danger and drama. The predictability, constancy, safety and security that depict many idealised notions of home[41] were rarely identified by this group.

Andrew's experiences are reflective of this. Andrew is a 23-year-old single male. He grew up in Melbourne's south-eastern suburbs and he was the second eldest of six children. Andrew's mother was addicted to heroin, as well as alcohol. Andrew had been physically abused on a number of occasions by his stepfather. Andrew had also been in foster care on numerous occasions. For Andrew it was the combined effects of being physically assaulted and having drug dependent parents that proved to be the catalyst:

> Mum had real problems with heroin and it got her in a heap of shit. Barry (his stepdad) was a fucking loser. He took advantage of her all the time.

Like Andrew, many of the escapers started to avoid going home, eventually staying out overnight to avoid the problems at home. This 'in and out' behaviour typically precedes a permanent break from home. Andrew's 'in and out' behaviour started when he was 13:

> You'd sleep in a clothes bin for a night. It was better than home.

When the problems at home got out of control Andrew would leave. In Andrew's eyes his mother didn't really:

> ... give a fuck man. I could've been dead and she wouldn't have known, probably wouldn't have cared either.

Apart from having to deal with physical abuse, Andrew was one of 10 people on the youth pathway who reported using heroin, speed or both before the onset of homelessness. All of these cases involved escapers who had been introduced to drugs by one or both parents (including de facto partners) or when they were under the care of statutory authorities. In Andrew's case his:

> ... mum and Barry were into smack. I'd been smoking dope since I was about 10 and by the time I was 13 I'd used smack. I even scored for them.

He also said that:

> Barry got me to carry some shit for him when we were in public ... he didn't want to get caught with smack on him so he got a fucking 14 year old to look after it.

Andrew's case highlights the complex and corrosive experiences that precede homelessness for many young people. One-quarter engaged in drug use before they became homeless but it occurred in a setting over which they had little control. When drug use is normal in family life or an institutional setting, young people are highly vulnerable.

This was also Robbie's experience. Robbie is 37. His mother died when he was two and his father was murdered when he was six. Robbie was put in the care of an uncle who sexually abused him when he was nine. Robbie was made a ward of the state and while in the care of the state he was physically and sexually abused. When he was 10 Robbie had his first encounter with the law and he has since developed a long history of custodial experiences. Robbie was in a juvenile justice facility when he was first introduced to smack. Drugs were 'a part of life' in these facilities and Robbie made the point that almost everyone was 'into it … it were impossible to avoid'.

While Robbie's is an extreme situation in many ways, in every case drugs, violence and the associated residential instability meant that their schooling suffered. For young people schooling is a primary connection to the mainstream. While low rates of high school completion were evident across most of the sample, problems at school had specific ramifications for escapers. Andrew thought it was:

> Fucking bizarre that I'd go to school after seeing me stepdad bash mum or I'd leave home and mum would be halfway blotted out already. You'd go to school and pretend everything was cool.

But he already felt an acute sense of difference between himself and the rest of his school friends:

> I'd see kids who had it easy complain about fucking anything. They had everything going for them. It made me sick.

Others felt isolated and stigmatised. Robbie found it a struggle to reconcile his home life with his school life:

> … one day I'd be totally out of it, you know, and the next I'd be in school sitting next to some twat who thought smoking was out there.

Toni found that when people discovered she had been, or was, in foster care she:

> Could say anything and it didn't matter a scrap. I was a foster kid and that said enough to most people. It made them uncomfortable.

In view of their own problems many escapers looked to other people who'd had similar experiences for support. This meant that rather than following the 'normal' pathway from school to work, this group had to negotiate identities that were developing in the context of violent, abusive or neglectful situations – situations that were not necessarily of their making yet situations that structured their subsequent actions. This created tension as 'normal' identities, while desired, appeared impossible to achieve. Andrew wished he:

Coulda stayed at school. I'd go along and listen to people talking about their lives and the problems they were having at home and all that and I'd think 'shit have they got it easy' ... I wanted to have what they did.

With few resources available to them, most eventually made a permanent break from home. When Andrew was abused in foster care he decided to leave for good. Surrounded by violence, denied access to mainstream institutions such as school and with life constantly in a state of flux, most found that the transition to homelessness was relatively seamless. Although there was some naivety about where to go and what to do, most were already 'streetwise'. For Toni, becoming homeless represented:

Another fuck-up in a long fucking line of them.

For Andrew the decision not to go back home raised mixed feelings for him. Relieved to be out of the fire he still:

... felt like I'd been shafted. I mean why the fuck was I homeless?

At one level the problems escapers had experienced at home made the transition to homelessness less problematic than for other groups. Nevertheless, life got even harder for all of these young people once they became homeless.

THE FIVE PATHWAYS

- Examination of five typical entry pathways into homelessness provides the empirical foundation upon which the connection between the *way* people become homeless and *what* subsequently happens to them can be established.

- While these entry pathways are ideal types, they demonstrate how individual biographies are reflexive in that individuals make decisions and choices. They also illustrate how those choices are shaped by external factors that in the main constrain the opportunities faced by people on the different pathways.

- There were distinct patterns of behaviour on each pathway, which reflected the different issues people had to deal with, the different biographies that people brought with them and the different structural factors they had to contend with. On each pathway the transition from housed to homeless disrupted people's routines, although the disruption was lived in diverse ways as people experienced external constraints in different ways.

- The primary connection between the five pathways was that everyone had few housing options because of their low income; poverty is at the centre of every experience of homelessness[41]. However, the findings warn against crude economic explanations. It is not accurate to say that economic structures on their own determine the processes through which people become homeless – these structures are important but their impact is mediated by other external factors and the biographies of individual actors.

- The five pathways reveal how different issues exert considerable influence on how the process of 'becoming homeless' unfolds. What they all show is how precariously balanced the 'ordinary' lives of poor people can be and how little it takes to tip a household over into the homeless population.

BEING HOMELESS

2 ON THE 'GO' – HOMELESS EXPERIENCES OF SUBSTANCE USERS

It is altogether curious, your first contact with poverty ... You thought it would be quite simple; it is extraordinarily complicated.

George Orwell, *Down and Out in Paris and London*

People with substance use issues tend to move quickly and easily into the homeless subculture. They typically manage the disruption to their lives by reconstructing routines within the homeless subculture, which has strong parallels to the social practices involved in 'using'. As a result they typically become entrenched in the homeless population. While there were frequent attempts to get out, these attempts generally failed. Stigma, combined with the survival routines of the homeless subculture, makes it hard to reconnect with the mainstream, and this ultimately perpetuates people's homelessness.

Stigma, subculture and routines all play important parts in the experience and duration of homelessness for this group. People on the substance use pathway face at least two kinds of stigma. The stigma of homelessness is compounded by the stigma of illegal substance use, evident in their experience of discrimination because of their appearance. Singled out by the physical signs of their prolonged drug use, these people often rearranged their routines to avoid the mainstream and preferred to engage with other homeless people. Consequently, the homeless subculture's strong 'present orientation' exerts a powerful influence on this group's experience of homelessness.

The experiences of this group also clarify another aspect of temporal order by showing that where criminal activity is reported, it generally occurs after homelessness.

IMPLICATIONS FOR CAREER DURATION

Of primary interest is to examine how people's experiences before and during homelessness influence the length of time they spend in the homeless population. The information on homeless duration in Table 2.1 shows the data converge in two clusters with people on the substance use, mental health and youth pathways reporting significantly longer experiences of homelessness than people on the domestic violence and housing crisis pathways.

Table 2.1 Temporal classification by pathway (per cent)

Pathway	Substance use (N=18)	Youth (N=41)	Mental health (N=6)	Domestic violence (N=14)	Housing crisis (N=24)	TOTAL (N=103)
Short term (0–3 months)	6	7	–	29 ⌉	46 ⌉	18 ⌉
Medium term (4–11 months)	6	3	17	43 ⌋ 72%	33 ⌋ 79%	17 ⌋ 35%
Long term (12+ months)	88	90	83	28	21	65
TOTAL	100	100	100	100	100	100
Mean months	55	41	73	7.5	8.5	33

Cluster one
Mean months 48

Cluster two
Mean months 8

People on the substance use pathway tended to remain homeless for significant periods of time. While there were frequent attempts to get out, these attempts had typically failed.

The duration of homelessness is strongly influenced by the way that prolonged drug use and frequent engagement with other homeless drug users produces a present orientation that makes it difficult to organise rehabilitation or arrange housing. People use the homelessness service system in a pragmatic way, and their experience demonstrates the critical role the homelessness service system plays in reproducing the homeless subculture.

Problematic substance use links people into the homeless subculture, which has its own specific survival routines and social practices. The research suggests that without immediate access to secure, affordable accommodation and support services the opportunity for successfully intervening in these careers is frequently lost.

SLIPPING INTO THE HOMELESS SUBCULTURE

The transition from housed to homeless was chaotic among individuals on the substance use pathway. There was, however, little evidence of the anxiety and stress that is commonly associated with becoming homeless. One possible reason is that most of this group were already involved in a using culture or what is sometimes called 'the scene'[1]. There is a clear overlap between the scene and the homeless subculture, and they both provide material support and a feeling of belonging – in a sense this group was already partially acculturated.

People on this pathway generally had a stable housing and employment history. Their transition into homelessness was a gradual process of losing their accommodation, staying with friends and finally using boarding houses, homelessness assistance agencies and squats, and also sleeping rough.

According to Milburn[2] people who use illicit substances commonly exploit close friends and family members and, as a result, many become alienated from them.

As these relationships collapsed, alternative social networks were forming and, by the time most people had lost their housing, they were linked in with the 'using culture'.

Without their own accommodation, and with no family to provide assistance, a common practice early on was to 'couch surf' between the homes of people who also had 'habits'. Keith's experience illustrates this clearly:

> I ended up staying with some friends for a couple of weeks. I didn't know them all that well ... they were, you know, part of the scene.

Similarly, in the first couple of months that John was homeless he tended to stay with people that he had:

> ... helped out with harry [heroin]. They were just a place to flop until something else came up.

Michelle made the point that when she was housed she had assisted people in much the same position.

Couch surfing is characterised by short stays as people regularly move from one place to another. The extent to which people couch surf is influenced by the size of their social networks but eventually everyone runs out of 'friends' to stay with. When this happens it is common to see people move into boarding houses (private lodgings and community rooming houses) often with financial assistance from welfare services. This marks an important stage in their homeless experience.

Although the initial stages of homelessness typically start with couch surfing, people soon begin to use boarding houses and welfare services and this is where many encounter the homeless subculture. In this social setting they start to learn the implicit rules and practices that structure interactions within the homeless subculture, including the widespread acceptance of substance use as a normal recreational activity.

When people cannot find a couch to crash on, boarding houses are one of the few accommodation options still available. Boarding houses accept week-by-week rental payments so that large sums of money are not required up front, and there are few, if any, reference checks. By this time most people have few possessions.

Like most people, Michelle was pragmatic about boarding houses. She:

> ... hated them, but I'd stay in 'em for a month or so until they kicked me out.

When she was kicked out, sometimes owing large amounts of rent, Michelle would start to 'do the circuit'. 'Doing the circuit' of boarding houses was common and it didn't take long before:

> You'd recognise a few faces and sometimes hook up with them.

Profiles of boarding house residents regularly portray a highly marginalised population with disproportionate levels of physical and mental health problems. Substance use problems are also commonly reported in studies from Australia and overseas[3-6].

It was in boarding houses that people met others in similar circumstances and this was the basis for the formation of new social networks. Although these networks were loose, regularly forming and dispersing, the crucial point is that boarding houses are a common locale through which a broad confluence of subcultural activity flows. Keith said that he just:

> … slipped into it. It was obvious there were heaps of people on the go. If you wanted something it wasn't hard to come by.

'Slipping into it' emphasises the relatively smooth transition for this group who, because of their experiences in the process of becoming homeless, had, to a certain extent, already been 'prepared' for the physical and social environment of boarding houses.

The transition from housed to homeless, while relatively smooth, was not without problems. John's opinion reflected the polarised attitudes towards boarding houses. Like others, John fluctuated between viewing boarding houses as 'shit holes' to the view that they were 'exciting' because they provided access to a range of social networks and activities:

> There was always something going on. You had to be on your toes though.

The homeless subculture is characterised by a 'here and now' orientation, which is similar to the 'here and now' orientation of the using culture. Recognising that both subcultures share a similar temporal orientation is vital in terms of understanding why people with drug dependencies are disproportionately represented among the long-term homeless.

REINVENTING ROUTINES

Living in the here and now

There are three interrelated sets of practices that shape the routines of homeless people with substance use problems: scoring, using and finding somewhere to sleep. These three factors create a 'present orientation'. When people have a present orientation it means that the contingencies of survival take precedence over future plans. The task of organising permanent housing – which in a tight housing market requires additional resources, planning, transport and luck to arrange – gets pushed to one side. As John said:

> Between trying to find a place for the night and getting gear it's fucking hard to do anything else.

With a focus on getting the next meal, getting money together, finding some accommodation and getting the next hit, thoughts about the long term were overwhelmed by what Snow and Anderson[7] describe as the 'consuming character of the immediate present'. Constantly waking up surrounded by the detritus of drug use, Keith said:

> … smack determined everything I did … it controlled me.

When asked about their future and about getting out of homelessness, an indication of this group's present orientation emerged. Only one-third thought that their drug problem would be resolved by the time they left transitional accommodation and only one-fifth had thought about their housing arrangements after transitional accommodation. In contrast, nearly two-thirds of the remaining people in the sample thought that their problems would be resolved by the time they left transitional housing, and most (71 per cent) had given some thought to where they would be going.

This is not to say that people on this pathway did not aspire to a conventional home or a job, or that they did not think about getting out of homelessness – they did.

In reality however, 'using', the social context in which it occurs and the routines that sustain it, typically limit the social and economic opportunities available to this group. Furthermore, repeated setbacks, violent experiences, poor health and low self-esteem tend to emphasise a future that holds little promise. With little sense of the future, priorities are increasingly located in the 'here and now', and are structured by social practices that are both physically and psychologically damaging. With little sense of the future, the chance of getting out of the homeless population is reduced. Once this cycle commences it is difficult to break.

Sharing resources

During the first interview it became apparent that friendships or associations with other homeless people and homeless drug users were very important in their daily routines. During the course of any day, interactions with other homeless people resulted in the sharing of resources. This could involve passing on information about services, what they offered, what they could and could not do or what individual workers were like, but it also included information about where to stay, where to get money and how to avoid 'the jacks' [the police]. Sharing resources in these ways is a key feature of the homeless subculture.

Resource sharing in the form of knowledge and information would pass from experienced homeless people to newcomers, as well as between friends and acquaintances. This information commonly formed the basis for many routines. When he was staying in one boarding house Keith found out:

> ... that most evenings a place down the road threw out unused food – bread mainly.

And, if he couldn't pay the rent at one boarding house, Keith was told that it was best to approach welfare agencies early in the week because that was when they:

> ... had more money available 'cause they'd run out by the end of the week.

This kind of knowledge formed the basis for discernable routines, and a level of continuity and predictability emerged from the instability of homelessness. John and his mate Joe would regularly:

> ... catch the tram into the city and get food from the Salvos. From there things would sorta work themselves out.

Keith knew that if he went for a meal at the local mission he would always find someone to 'hook up with'.

Information also filtered through a loose network of boarding house residents. One time when Keith was in the Miami, a notorious inner city boarding house:

> … word came around there were cleaning jobs available at Colonial
> Stadium [a nearby football stadium] … by the time I got there it
> looked like half the Miami was there …

It was also common to see people at Centrelink. Michelle went to Centrelink frequently, and commented that after:

> … we had filled in a few forms, a few of us would go chasing
> [looking to score drugs].

Sharing resources included implicit, though not necessarily consistent information, about the rules that 'govern' the homeless subculture. Robbie, from the youth pathway, recounted that when he first started sleeping out people tried to 'protect him' by telling him 'how it worked' and what 'not to do'.

Raising money

The 'euphoria of using' constituted only part of each day. What predominantly structured the day and shaped many social interactions was what Rowe[8] terms 'the business of raising money'. This 'business' dominated people's day-to-day lives because the cost of illicit drugs is so high that people on low incomes had to devote large amounts of time to securing money. The result was that everything else tended to fall by the wayside. For Andrew it was still the case that:

> Pretty much from the moment I wake up I think about getting gear, about how I can get some money and score.

People employed a range of strategies to raise the money they needed to survive and, at the same time, maintain their habit. Some shoplifted, while others talked about the scams they would pull to get money. Many of these scams were learnt from other homeless people in the course of hanging around with them. Keith mentioned that:

> You'd spend a lot of the time hanging around and you'd hear about what was happening … heaps of it was bullshit of course, but you'd hear some good stuff.

John learnt the '$50 trick' from a bloke in a crisis accommodation facility. The trick involved asking a shop attendant to change a $50 bill – when the shop attendant offered the change you grabbed it and 'ran as fast as you could'. The scam worked for John until he went back to a store he had scammed previously:

> This bloke eyed me off for a while, and when I pulled out a $50 bill his face froze … I knew immediately that something was wrong and bolted.

The $50 trick was just one of many scams. Others did work as drivers or lookouts on burglaries; some would 'do houses' themselves; while others turned to sex work. Significantly though, most people did not see themselves as criminals. They viewed these crimes as a result of the cost of heroin and their low income. Michelle was angered by this:

> If smack didn't cost so much I wouldn't have done some of the shit
> things I done.

By using an illegal drug, people in this group were criminalised and further marginalised because they engaged in illegal activities to get the money they required to support their drug dependency.

Over time people started to specialise and this was, to a certain extent, mediated by their age and their gender. Keith did 'burgs' (burglaries) while Michelle started to 'lay in the car' – meaning she worked as a street prostitute using her clients' cars. This was extremely risky and Michelle knew one working girl that had been killed. Although men did turn to sex work, it was confined to a minority of younger men.

The most common way to get money was to deal in drugs. Michelle said she 'started selling to get by … little bits here and there'. While some people had 'dealt' prior to becoming homeless it was much more common for people to start dealing once they were homeless. For many, there was a clear crossover between their role as a user and as a dealer. Early on it was mainly small-scale dealing and because they were easy to rip off it was common to hear stories of 'fresh faces' being targeted. John was up front about how he would prey on new 'green' kids. At one level he would help them, and gain their trust, by sharing resources and information that helped them cope with homelessness. But he also took advantage of them. John knew that 'drugs were the key ... they were seen as cool'.

For people like John, dealing commonly lead to increased consumption and this was a 'big mistake'. When John got some heroin on 'tick' [credit] and 'blasted' [injected] it up his arm, he thought he would be able to 'cover my arse', but couldn't do so. One morning while he was staying at a boarding house he was woken by a loud:

> ... fuckin' crash and then there's a fuckin' gun at my head. That's frightening man, you don't want that to happen too often.

John reflected that whereas previously he would have 'done anything' to get his fix, after the incident with the gun he played it much smarter – 'by the rules'. Similarly Keith was reminded that dealing was not a particularly safe activity, particularly when on one occasion he cut the gear 'too heavily'. After selling it he:

> ... copped a hiding. I thought they were fresh faces and wouldn't know.

These experiences taught them much.

Even though drug use and dealing can spill over into the public domain creating occasional moral panics[9], using is generally hidden from public view and much of what happens occurs out of sight of the authorities and the public. In an unregulated market this means, of course, that when problems arise, typically around quantity or quality, there is no recourse other than violence. Nevertheless the homeless subculture has rules to govern social interactions.

Playing by the rules

These examples reveal some of the structure of the homeless subculture. On one level the homeless subculture appears fluid and chaotic and this creates the impression that the subculture has no real form or structure. Yet the existence of rules that regulate behaviour, albeit loosely, indicates that the homeless subculture shapes the social practices of many homeless people. As Giddens[10] points out, to perform a social practice 'participants must necessarily draw on a set of rules; these rules can be seen to give structure to the practices they help to organise'.

Over time, the 'rules' became routinised practices as the knowledge and information that shaped day-to-day life was passed from the experienced to the inexperienced and from friend to friend.

This is the way that the homeless subculture regenerates or reproduces itself. Although subcultural practices may be loosely defined, often implied and commonly contradictory, they nevertheless provide a degree of structure and coherence to the day-to-day lives of many homeless people. The rules provide an implicit context for people's behaviours and interactions. They are revealed in the consequences when individuals accidentally, or wilfully, break or bend them.

Like most cultural norms, the rules of the homeless subculture are not published anywhere or maintained by anyone in particular. This means that people are particularly vulnerable to the risks of transgression early in their homeless experience.

John knew he was 'lucky to survive' a number of incidents as a result of unknowingly breaking the rules. Not knowing the rules could get you into serious trouble. Keith recalled the time he saw a young fellow assaulted by a group of boarding house residents. The young fellow had:

> ... done the wrong thing and got what was coming to him – he'd fucked up big time.

Keith had also found out about the rules the hard way. He was attacked and, for a short time, ostracised for stealing from a room at a boarding house. Ripping off other people is a common practice in the homeless subculture, but there is a subtle etiquette and unless you follow the rules the results can be undesirable. Keith was assaulted because the room he broke into contained a family and this transgressed the unwritten rule that you:

> Leave families alone ... it's the kids you see. People who fuck around with children are the lowest.

When Keith 'rolled a crazy' at the same place, 'no one gave a fuck'. As people became more involved with the homeless subculture, some, like John, got involved in violent crime. While it brought higher rewards the risks were greater:

> When we knocked over a dealer the word was out on the street fuckin' quickly. You have to know how to keep quiet otherwise you're fucked.

While cases like this were rare and were sometimes part of an elaborate fiction, they draw attention to the point that as people's dependency increases it leads to more desperate measures to secure money. As people became more deeply embedded in the homeless subculture, they became less fearful, rules were flouted and their perception of themselves began to change. At this point it was common to see things spiral out of control. John got to the point where he was:

> Doing crazy things, fucking crazy things. When this cunt put a knife to my face I told him to stab me because I was already fucking dead.

CRIME AND THE STREETS

There is both evidence and a common perception that crime, homelessness and illegal substance use are linked, but there is considerable contention about the nature of the relationship[11-13]. This research found that 23 per cent of the sample had been incarcerated at some time in their lives. However, it was clear that criminal activity was primarily a response to the contingencies of homelessness and the high cost of illegal drugs, with 68 per cent of those who engaged in criminal activity reporting that it occurred after they became homeless.

There was also significant variation by pathway. For instance, no one on the domestic violence pathway reported criminal activity, while people on the substance use pathway were over twice as likely to have been incarcerated, with 55 per cent reporting that they had been incarcerated at some point in their lives. However, eight of the 10 people on this pathway who had been incarcerated spent time in prison after they had experienced homelessness. This is consistent with the view that among homeless people most criminal activity is primarily an adaptive response.

There are two important factors shaping the correlation between substance use, crime and homelessness. First, prohibition plays a key role in keeping the price of heroin high; much of the crime linked to heroin and other illicit drugs could be avoided if people had access to legal and affordable drugs. Second, homeless people, particularly visible groups like substance users, are likely to attract police attention and this can increase rates of incarceration for activities not necessarily linked to substance use or homelessness.

Keith recounted how at one time he was:

> ... fined for not having a train ticket. When they asked for my address I told them I didn't have one. It got out of control and they called the cops.

Over time some people cycled between homelessness and prison and this became a feature of their lives. Over 80 per cent of those who had been imprisoned had been so more than once. Drugs generally underpinned the cycle, but it was exacerbated by a lack of affordable and appropriate accommodation to exit to and a lack of support once they were out[14-16]. John, who was on a bond for possession, was put inside for six months after he was caught robbing a house. When John left prison he went straight back to the streets:

> They opened the doors and pushed me out. I went straight back and 'got on' [used heroin] that afternoon.

Few people left prison with their heroin problems addressed or with much thought given to their housing needs.

USING HOMELESSNESS SERVICES

While scoring, using and raising money play a vital role in shaping daily routines, finding a place to stay also consumes a great deal of time. Along with boarding houses, the homelessness service system is another institution through which people encounter the homeless subculture, and it plays an important role in the dynamics of people's homeless careers. Seventy-five per cent of the group reported that they had previously been in transitional accommodation. However, there was variation in the use of the homelessness service system across the five pathways and the data converge in two clusters.

The first cluster is comprised of three pathways (substance use, mental health and youth). In this cluster 95 per cent of the respondents had previously been housed in transitional accommodation. In the second cluster (housing crisis and domestic violence) the pattern was significantly different with approximately 40 per cent reporting that they had been in transitional accommodation previously.

Many respondents on the substance use pathway mentioned that they had also used crisis facilities regularly. Transitional accommodation was harder to get, but this was actively sought as well. 'Getting a place' was 'part of the game' and Michelle said it was well known on the street that to get accommodation you sometimes had to play a role. The longer you spent in the homeless population the more knowledgeable you became about welfare organisations and the more skilled you became at crafting a story:

> You'd swear all of these things. That you were going to do this, that you were going to do that, just to get some money or a place where you could hit up.

The paradox of 'making up stories' was obvious to Michelle who found it was 'weird given our lives were so fucked up that we had to make up stories'.

Without understanding the material constraints that homeless people face, patterns of repeatedly using welfare services and the practice of 'telling stories' are commonly presented by conservative commentators such as Saunders[17] as dependence on, or abuse of, the welfare system. However, when this behaviour is examined in its resource depleted context there is a clear rationality that has little to do with welfare dependency or personality defects.

Perhaps the most incisive comment relates to the putative restorative function of the homelessness service system. Keith said that:

When you've got nothing – no money, no accommodation, no hope
of getting a job – you have to [tell stories]. They presume you want
to give up. They just don't understand it's just not like that.

This draws attention to how drug dependency redefines
relationships with non-users, as well as with the housing and
labour markets. These relationships do not change or revert to
normal immediately after a person stops using.

As many people would find, when they were 'clean' they
would have to fight against the effects of long absences from
the workforce, a poor rental history and coming to terms with
having few, if any, social connections in the mainstream. These
factors are significant barriers to getting out and staying out of
the homeless population.

Over time it was clear that accessing welfare services became
a normal part of day-to-day life, or a routinised practice.

The data indicate that most people on this pathway had
been in transitional accommodation on multiple occasions.
Overall, there was a pattern of multiple stays in transitional
accommodation although, once again, the data converge in two
distinct clusters. The first cluster includes the substance use, youth
and mental health pathways. People on these pathways had been
in transitional accommodation, on average, five times. This is
nearly three times the level found among people on the domestic
violence and housing crisis pathways (mean times housed 1.8).

Some people on the substance use pathway found it difficult
to stabilise their situation while they were in emergency
accommodation. This was because of the link it maintained

to other homeless people and the homeless subculture. John's experience illustrates this:

> I moved in with Ned and as I got to know him and we started to do stuff together ... we eventually got kicked out because they found some 'fits' [syringes] in the place.

The third time John was accommodated he was 'really desperate to get clean'. Trying to stay clean was hard enough, but he had to share, once again, with a person who was still using. Not surprisingly John found that:

> ... just being around 'harry' [heroin] was too much. Within a month or so I was back to where I was before I moved in.

Similarly, in Michelle's case, rather than helping her to get out, her experiences of emergency accommodation also maintained her connection to the homeless subculture. Michelle's current transitional property was 'well known' and people would 'drop in all the time' and she thought the whole thing was:

> ... laughable, this place is right in the heart of the action.

In these instances, transitional accommodation could perpetuate substance use rather than disrupt it.

Sleeping rough

The longer people remained homeless, the more likely they were to start sleeping rough. The use of squats, for instance, is common among homeless people with a drug dependency[18]. Keith commented that:

> ... squats were good because they were private. You could get on and not worry so much.

At the same time squats could expose people to all sorts of dangers. John said that when they found a squat:

> You'd try and keep it quiet but word would get around pretty quickly.

And that squats could quickly turn into:

> ... shooting galleries ... there were thousands of fits on the ground at my last squat. It was fucking full on at times, what with everyone looking to 'get on' all the time.

And Michelle, who used squats less frequently, said that when squats got well known:

> We'd move from squat to squat – sometimes the coppers would leave us alone, other times they'd raid us.

And that:

> There could be 20 people in a single squat ... they weren't all users either. There'd be some old fellas and some nutters, but mainly it was junkies though.

A number of women mentioned that they tried to avoid squats by moving in with men, a practice commonly known as 'shacking up'[77].

Even though shacking up was aimed at providing security and shelter, it tended to reinforce their vulnerability. Michelle said that she:

> ... hooked up with Terry because I had nowhere to stay ... I'd known him for a while as we often scored together.

Although shacking up provided a roof over her head, it also put Michelle at risk of violence and exploitation. One day Terry turned on Michelle:

> ... in a violent rage and beat me up so bad I got taken to hospital.

When people could not find somewhere to sleep, sleeping rough was a common response and virtually everyone (89 per cent) reported that they had slept rough at some point in their homeless careers (Table 2.2). Again, the data converge in two clusters with the people on the substance use, mental health and youth pathways all reporting similarly high rates of sleeping rough.

Table 2.2 Reports of sleeping rough by onset pathway (per cent)

Pathway	Substance use (N=18)	Youth (N=41)	Mental health (N=6)	Domestic violence (N=14)	Housing crisis (N=24)	TOTAL (N=103)
Slept rough	89	71	83	14	21	55

| | Cluster one | Cluster two |
| | 77 per cent | 18 per cent |

In contrast, the incidence of sleeping rough reported among people on the domestic violence and housing crisis pathways was approximately a quarter of the rate of the first cluster. The variation in the reported rates of sleeping rough highlights the way that different patterns of social interaction and different social practices can emerge from within the same broad set of structural factors. This point further emphasises the active role that individuals play in interpreting their situation in ways that make sense to them.

For many people who have a drug dependency it is not the focus on 'using' that leads to sleeping rough. Sleeping rough typically occurs as a result of acute social and economic resource depletion.

Although using occasionally took precedence over accommodation, sleeping rough generally happened only after people had unsuccessfully tried to access crisis accommodation or rehabilitation services but were unable to because they were full[20] or there were waiting lists[21].

Homeless people with a drug dependency find themselves at the very bottom of the housing market.

MANAGING STIGMA

Stigma was a significant non-material structure shaping the experience of people on the substance use pathway. They had to manage the dual stigma of being homeless and being drug dependent*.

---

* Incarceration would also complicate the experience of stigma for some on this pathway.

Homelessness is associated with particular images – bad body smell and dishevelled appearance are among the enduring images of skid row that continue to resonate in the public mind. Stereotypes commonly associated with long-term substance abuse include poor skin, rotting teeth, sallow complexion and track marks. These are overt, visual symbols that carry social information about people and mark them as 'social outcasts' or outsiders.

People on this pathway found that increasing amounts of time on the street and long-term drug use did impact on their health status and their physical appearance. These changes to their health status are significant in terms of understanding their homeless careers, and were particularly noticeable when there was a heroin drought and people turned to other drugs, such as speed. For two people, their mental health problems emerged as a consequence of extended drug use. During one such dry spell Keith noticed a number of users who went on 'speed benders' and 'lost the plot'. Others used drugs such as temazepam and the physical impact was shocking. John witnessed the results of injecting temazepam and commented that:

> I won't shoot that shit up, no fucking way man. I know one bloke who lost a couple of fingers.

The physical effects of long-term drug use also included malnourishment, hepatitis C and missing teeth. These overt signs marked them out as 'junkies' and it was the physical signs of drug use that created the most problems when interacting with the mainstream. Michelle said that at times she 'felt invisible' and that people looked right 'through her'. Michelle was shocked when she saw some:

> ... photos. I didn't recognise myself at first. I looked so old.

In their interactions with the mainstream, homeless people with substance use problems attributed the discrimination they encountered to the physical signs of their dependency. These visual cues shaped other people's reactions and underpinned much of the discrimination that they encountered. Michelle said that every time she went to the supermarket or a department store 'they'd check my bags out'. Similarly, John said that at one time he was reluctant to go out because every time he did it felt like the 'cops pull me over because of the way I look. They think I'm usin' or holdin'. The way this group looked and what it 'said about them' exerted a significant influence on the nature of their interactions with the mainstream.

As a result of routinely encountering discriminatory practices, people develop routines to avoid situations where this might happen. This tends to cement existing social relationships within the homeless subculture.

The discrimination they experience is not about their physical attributes *per se*, but is shaped by the social identity attached to illicit drug use and the relationship of that social identity to mainstream normative structures. Being a homeless drug user is a socially devalued identity in that it implies a rejection of mainstream values and practices.

The overt physical signs of drug use provided information that enabled people to formalise their discrimination in a quick and remarkably consistent fashion, a process described by Link and Phelan[22] as a form of 'cognitive efficiency'. Keith experienced this cognitive efficiency when he applied for a rental property:

> I'm sure they just threw the application in the bin. The woman behind the counter took one look at me and that was it.

Identifying with other homeless people

The longer people remain in the homeless population, the more likely they are to identify with homelessness as 'a way of life'.

Identification with homelessness was further strengthened by the fact that as people became embedded in the homeless subculture most lost contact with the 'normal' world. Over time the compounding impact of repeated rejections, discrimination and poor self-image resulted in people finding support from others who'd had similar experiences. In this way their social networks were increasingly comprised of other homeless people. Michelle found some solace in the fact that:

> At least other homeless people know how hard it is … I feel better with them because they don't put me down … they know the shit I been through.

John's thoughts echoed the same theme:

> They [other homeless people] don't stare down at you … they understand what it's like and don't judge you because of it.

For Michelle, John and others, the homeless subculture can provide support and a sense of belonging.

Over time connections to the homeless subculture strengthen and increasingly shape day-to-day social interactions. As a result many of the social practices we've described become routinised. The homeless subculture and the routines that support it provide, on the one hand, meaning and purpose but, on the other, create an ongoing tension between belonging to a group and exploiting the very group they 'belong to'.

Negotiating the tension between the supportive and the predatory elements of the homeless subculture eventually wore people down, and reduced the desire to get out.

While the homeless subculture provided some support, security and a degree of personal validation, it was limited and partial; ultimately, homelessness was a deeply destructive experience. Many were engulfed by nihilism, anomie and anger. John, who had been homeless for six years, 'didn't give a fuck' because he knew that whatever happened, he had 'been there already'. Keith, who had 'been through it all', said, 'why complain? It all stays the same'. Like most of the people on this pathway, Keith, Michelle and John had become chronically homeless and for them getting out and staying out of homelessness would prove to be difficult, but not impossible.

THE SUBSTANCE USE PATHWAY

- People who become homeless because of substance use typically become entrenched in the homeless population. Most people on this pathway moved into the homeless subculture quickly because they were already involved in 'the scene'.

- The 'using scene' has many overlaps with the homeless subculture, including a focus on the 'here and now' which makes it difficult to organise, or focus on, housing or work, and many in the group resorted to illegal activities to raise the money they needed to get by. As these practices became part of people's daily routines there was a strong identification with other drug-using homeless people and an acceptance of homelessness as a way of life. These social practices are mediated through a complex interaction of depleted housing options, the socioeconomic treatment of narcotics as illicit drugs and how individuals make sense of, and remake, their devalued social identities.

- In trying to illuminate the nexus between substance use and homelessness, explanations have shown an implicit tendency to characterise homeless people with substance abuse problems as either inadequate or flawed, or to link substance use to self-medication in response to mental health problems or early life trauma. While these issues exist for some homeless people, it is important to realise that overall this group has extensive social networks. They collaborate in joint activities, and many positively identify with homelessness as a way of life.

- Without romanticising the life of homeless drug users, accounts that characterise this group as passive, dependent or isolated are inadequate.

- This chapter describes the group of people whose substance use problems occurred prior to becoming homeless. As will be shown in subsequent chapters, people who become homeless because of substance use represent only one-quarter of those who report substance use problems. In fact the majority of homeless drug-dependent people in this study developed substance use problems *after* they had experienced homelessness.

3 HOMELESS CAREERS OF THE MENTALLY ILL

I walk the streets aimlessly, as if merely moving can alleviate the suffering of consciousness ... This is the old lostness from before, the last time; depression is coming on now, will wipe me out. Panic precedes depression, heralds it. It is the pointless frantic energy before lethargy, a last attempt to effect something through motion. All I think about is money ... Now it is just survival, how to make it through the next few months. There is always the deadline of poverty.

Kate Millet, *The Loony Bin Trip*

It is important to consider the way in which the actions of the people on the mental health pathway are shaped by the structural properties of the housing and labour markets, in order to make the connection between this group's experiences leading to homelessness and their experiences of homelessness.

The way in which people with mental health problems respond to and reproduce the stigma of homelessness is different to the ways homeless people on the substance use pathway do. Homeless people with mental health problems set up different day-to-day routines, which result in a different experience of homelessness and of getting out and staying out of homelessness.

The people on this pathway managed their entry into the homeless population with few, if any, social networks. Most ended up in boarding houses early on in their careers where they often encountered violence and intimidation. Two actions this group take to minimise their vulnerability are to frequently move between boarding houses and to withdraw from social contact. In the process of withdrawing they invert the 'homeless' hierarchy to create their own social order. These actions result in routines that reproduce the conditions that maintain and sustain their marginalisation.

People who enter the homeless population because of mental health problems have the longest and most isolated experience of homelessness. However, this group does not identify with other homeless people or homelessness as a way of life.

ABRUPT BREAK

In the process of becoming homeless, the six individuals who had mental health problems had lost most of their possessions and had been uprooted from their social environment with few social or economic resources. While this was happening they also had to manage their health problems. Unlike the initial entry into homelessness for people on the substance use pathway, which was buffered by their existing networks in 'the scene', people with mental health problems had few social networks at this point. This, combined with the ongoing denial of their health problems, meant that their homelessness usually began with an abrupt break.

For some people in this group their homeless careers began by sleeping rough. One person noted how after a fortnight on the beach he became increasingly concerned for his safety. Where Tim had been sleeping wasn't:

> ... far from a spot where a bunch of people drank at night. You'd hear them going on, but it was the fighting that got me.

Although he felt unsafe, Tim's main recollection was that he was overwhelmed by feelings of 'anger and frustration'. These feelings, in combination with his rejection of the labels 'mentally ill' and 'homeless', reduced his desire to seek assistance.

The more common pattern, however, was to move directly into boarding houses and this created its own problems. Maggie recalled the first night she spent in a boarding house:

> ... the noise and the smell of urine and vomit. It was terribly frightening. It had this awful vibe about it, it's hard to explain but, well, I spent the night waiting for the morning to come.

In the initial stages of their homeless careers, people had to deal with the anxiety of having nowhere safe or permanent to stay. Feelings of alienation and isolation were compounded by the fact that there was little predictability or permanency in their lives. Initially, boarding houses were viewed as temporary accommodation and even after a couple of months Maggie recalled that she kept on hoping that it 'would get better. I didn't expect to spend so much time there'. The sense that boarding houses were a temporary option contributed to the problem of establishing day-to-day routines.

With no continuity and little predictability in their daily lives, accommodation problems were exacerbated by the fact that the cost of living in boarding houses consumed a large part of their income. Because of their poor position in the labour market everyone relied on government benefits. With the cost of a room or a dormitory bed in boarding houses ranging from $120–160 a week, people were spending over 50 per cent of their income on substandard accommodation*. This made it impossible to save money to secure better accommodation. Maggie's frustration was clearly evident:

> I'd spend nearly all of my pension on these shit holes. Some were meant to provide food. I tell you it's not food … one place used newspaper in the toilet.

Apart from their high costs it was common to hear stories of places 'full of bedbugs' and 'cockroaches', rotten food, unhygienic conditions and the remains of drug use. It is also well known that boarding houses can be unsafe places to live in[1].

MARGINALISATION

Studies of boarding house residents have reported that people with mental health problems are frequently taken advantage of by other residents[2].

---

* The two primary sources of government income were Newstart (N=1) and the Disability Support Pension (DSP) (N=5). Newstart payments are $202.25 per week; DSP payments are $244.45 per week. Source: centrelink.gov.au/internet/internet.nsf/payments/

Tim, who found his own way into a boarding house within a month of becoming homeless, recalled that on his second night:

> A couple knocked on my door and asked for some cigarettes. They sort of moved into the room and pinched my wallet. The thing was I didn't see them again and was never sure if they lived there or not.

In the early stages of their homeless careers Tim and Maggie reported that they were preyed on by other residents who often had drug problems. Boarding house residents often target the mentally ill, exploiting their loneliness and desire for social contact. Tim spoke of other experiences in boarding houses that further emphasised his vulnerability:

> You had to be alert … those friggin' junkies would pinch anything. I lost a radio and a backpack and my food was always being taken.

Maggie witnessed a number of violent situations and frequently felt intimidated by other residents. At one boarding house two male residents approached her:

> … making obscene gestures and that sort of stuff … I felt very afraid 'cause they knew my room where I was living.

Some landlords also took advantage of this group's vulnerability. At one place when Tim reported to the landlord that the shower was not working:

> … he (the landlord) told me I could go and live anywhere I wanted to. Meaning shut up or fuck off.

At another place Tim had to pay a $50 key deposit and when he left the landlord refused to return it, claiming it was 'to clean my room'.

This group responded in two distinct ways to the social practices of landlords and other residents. The first response was to try to find better accommodation. The second response was to withdraw from social situations where they felt vulnerable.

First, this group regularly moved between boarding houses throughout their homeless careers, although the pattern was more pronounced in the early stages. Moving between places rarely resulted in improved living conditions and often created additional problems. Frequent changes of address meant that Centrelink* obligations were regularly missed and for those not on the Disability Support Pension (DSP) this led to problems with income payments. Tim's payments had been reduced on two previous occasions because he had failed to turn up for appointments. Fluctuating health problems made maintaining appointments difficult and this meant that Tim was punished because of the very problem that caused him to require support and income assistance in the first place:

> ... they (Centrelink staff) didn't want to help at all. Well, it sort of got out of control from that point and, well, anyway I ended up without any money and couldn't pay rent.

Another result of frequent moving was that it took them into areas where they had few social connections. Links with

---

* Centrelink is an Australian government agency that delivers a range of services to the community. A primary service is providing income support to the unemployed, people with disabilities, low-income families and people over 65 years of age.

mental health services that had been established in one region were often difficult to transfer to another area and as a result they commonly lapsed. When this happened it was common for people to stop taking their medication altogether and this tended to exacerbate their mental health problems. Despite disclaimers about her health, Maggie acknowledged that she found it hard when she stopped taking her medication:

> There was no one to help me when it got out of control and I'd generally end up in trouble when it happened.

As people cycled in and out of hospital, maintaining accommodation was frequently compromised. Maggie reported that:

> One time I was in [psychiatric hospital] for nearly two months. When I got out I went back to the Royal [a boarding house] but all my stuff had been given away. There was nothing I could do.

When they were discharged they often had nowhere to go, and would end up on the street looking for boarding house accommodation.

As boarding house numbers decline there is additional pressure on vulnerable people to accept 'unacceptable conditions'. The second response to the violence and exploitation of the boarding house environment is to withdraw from social contact.

Maggie tried to blend in with her surroundings and make herself as unobtrusive as possible:

> There were certain times I'd make myself scarce … payday was always crazy and I learnt to avoid junkies who were hanging out.

Tim found that if he:

> ... stayed quiet, no one would bother me ... there was always noise, but I avoided it.

The process of withdrawing changed the way this group interacted with both material and non-material structures. For instance, relationships in the housing and labour markets were virtually non-existent and this led to their reliance on boarding houses for accommodation. Once they were in boarding houses they withdrew further to avoid victimisation and exploitation.

Previous accounts of the process of 'withdrawing' among homeless people have relied on Robert Merton's[3] idea of retreatism which 'arises from the continued failure' to achieve socially sanctioned goals. He goes on to say that continued failure leads to 'Defeatism, quietism and resignation [that] are manifested in escape mechanisms which ultimately lead him to "escape" from the requirements of society'.

However, the process of withdrawal and the resulting social isolation has little to do with failure to achieve socially approved goals. Instead, other homeless people, especially users, take advantage of the mentally ill, which leads to their withdrawing. Patterns of interaction are strongly influenced by the fact that individual actors recognise their own vulnerability and, in trying to minimise it, perpetuate their vulnerability. Also, although there is always variation in the way people respond to individuals who have mental health issues, it is not uncommon for the mentally ill to be exploited by other homeless people.

STIGMA AND THE SOCIAL HIERARCHY

Within the homeless population there is considerable variation in how other homeless people are viewed. These different views form the basis of a social hierarchy within the homeless population. While there was strong identification with other homeless people among some groups, there was also a clear stratification of the homeless population based on what Goffman[4] identified as 'the attitudes the normals take'.

Keith, who became homeless because of substance use, had spent a lot of time in boarding houses. He commented on the 'crazies' and the 'nutters' who would spend all day:

> Laughing and talking to themselves ... there was always a few of
> them in any of the boarding houses I've stayed in.

Similarly Toni, who shared a transitional house with another young woman, thought people with mental health problems were 'fuck-ups'.

These responses from homeless people towards other homeless people who had mental health problems highlight two issues. First, they reaffirm that 'mental illness is one of the most stigmatised conditions'[5]. Second, they show that homeless people stratify the homeless population and place the mentally ill at the bottom of the scale.

People on the mental health pathway were acutely aware of these attitudes. The lack of interaction and identification with other homeless people was a uniform characteristic of this group.

When asked if they had anything in common with the homeless, only one person said he did. These attitudes were also evident in their efforts to manage their identity. Whereas identification with the homeless was high for those on the substance use pathway, only one person on the mental health pathway reported that they identified with other homeless people, and only two people described themselves as homeless.

This is consistent with other findings that show that people with mental health problems have fewer social networks than do other people[6-8].

Instead of identifying with other homeless people, people on the mental health pathway inverted the social hierarchy. Tim believed that the other residents 'deserved the place ... they were only interested in drinking or drugs anyway'. To make sense of their isolation, the inversion of the homeless hierarchy is an important social practice, and they drew on and reinterpreted stereotypes of the homeless to do this. Maggie thought that her problems would vanish if she could 'find a better place and get away from these people'. This group actively differentiated themselves from other homeless people by denying their own problems and emphasising the flaws of others.

ENTRENCHMENT AND AVOIDANCE

By minimising their direct involvement with other homeless people it could be assumed that this group would show few signs of adapting to the homeless subculture where drug and alcohol use, and the business of raising money, were a part of day-to-day life. The research showed this assumption to be partially correct – no one developed alcohol problems, only one person reported a period of incarceration after they became homeless and two people reported that they began to use drugs after they became homeless. In both instances it appears that drugs were a form of self-medication used to 'blot out the day', and these two people moved in and out of the homeless subculture – sometimes engaging with it, and at other times withdrawing from it. The more common experience was to avoid the homeless subculture altogether.

Using, scoring and the business of raising money gives structure and coherence to the day-to-day lives of people on the substance use pathway. Among people on the mental health pathway, what gives structure to their daily lives is the way they respond to their exclusion from the mainstream and to the intimidation, abuse and threats from other homeless people. It is important to stress that it is not their health issues that create problems, but the way those problems are interpreted by other homeless people and form the basis for distinct forms of social action by others.

New routines

People with mental health problems rebuilt their routines in different ways to other homeless people. Routines were commonly constructed around agencies that provide food and material relief. People with mental health problems relied on these agencies more heavily than any other group. Everyone on this pathway used material aid services in the month preceding the first interview at least once. This contrasts with the overall rate across the sample of 44 per cent.

Circuits of these agencies formed an important part of their daily routines. The importance of these agencies extended beyond the material assistance they offered and was tied to the fact that they provided a safe haven and a fixed reference point. Apart from the security of knowing these agencies were there for them, the use of these services was part of a strategy directed towards 'fill[ing] in the day'. When he was well, Tim would spend 'many hours' in the library 'doing research'. At other times he would ride trains all day to stay warm and 'look at the city'. Similarly, Maggie fed the ducks at the local park every day and she worried constantly over who would look after them if she wasn't around. In fact, it was clear that everyone carved out social space where they felt in control and with that came unique and important routines.

Although these routines brought the mentally ill into contact with other people, both housed and homeless, there was rarely any sustained interaction. While the routines of people on the mental health pathway enabled them to create their own space and endure homelessness, these routines tended to entrench them in their current circumstances.

While food and material relief agencies were regularly used, there was little contact with office based housing or support services. While all of the respondents in this group had previously been in transitional accommodation – on average, three times – support agencies were used less often compared to the substance use group who had previously been accommodated, on average, four times.

One explanation for the low level of service utilisation relative to the length of their homeless careers is that many support services are unable to cope with people who have mental health problems. There was evidence to support this contention as five of the six people on this pathway reported that they had been barred from a service at one stage or another.

There has been much debate in recent years about increasing complexity in the homeless population and the exclusion of certain homeless groups by agencies funded to assist the homeless[9]. This debate has typically been framed in terms of 'service-resistant' or 'complex' clients. In the US some researchers have suggested that it has more to do with 'service-resistant service providers'. In his study of 50 chronically homeless people with mental health problems in Los Angeles, Paul Koegel[10] observed that they were:

> ... struck, as have been others, by the extent to which people dismissed as service-resistant do want services but, in seeking them, have failed to get what they want and thus do not return, or have found that services are set such that accessing them is too difficult, too costly or too frustrating. When one includes all these contextual factors in the analysis, it becomes possible to talk about 'service-resistant service providers' and 'service-resistant service settings', rather than simply 'service-resistant clients'.

Maggie's experiences suggest that she had encountered the sort of 'service-resistant service providers' Koegal was referring to. When a housing service arranged and paid for accommodation at a local boarding house, which Maggie described as abysmal, she was annoyed by the attitude of the workers who made out they were 'doing you a favour'. Maggie soon realised that many services were 'quick to judge and slow to understand'. Maggie reported that it was easier to avoid these services, rather than suffer the indignity of being treated like a 'no hoper'.

MAKING SENSE AND ACCEPTANCE

The accommodation biographies of this group revealed decreasing movement between boarding houses the longer they spent in the homeless population.

With few, if any, housing or employment options, there was an increasing acceptance of their housing situation. Tim said:

> On a good day it was OK. If I was feeling well I could mange it and it wasn't so bad. But when things got bad, you know when I was ill, or, well it was harder, it was difficult to cope.

And as he got used to boarding houses he began to arrange his day around the rhythm of boarding house life:

> It [the bathroom] didn't worry me as much. There was no one around at 10:00 [am] and so I'd go then. It was cleaner then as well.

One-fifth of the sample had spent six months or more living in the same boarding houses but, amongst people on the mental health pathway, everyone had lived in a boarding house for at least six months at some point. This implies that this group had come to accept living in boarding houses more easily than did other groups.

Importantly, the decision to treat boarding houses as a permanent accommodation option did not occur because people started to like these places. As housing opportunities diminished, people internalised their new relationship to the housing market, which was then reflected in the changing perception of boarding houses as a temporary accommodation option to a permanent one.

These cognitive changes were also underpinned by an emerging sense that normal life was being denied to them. For homeless people with mental health issues, their sense of self-worth was often compromised by their health problems and the social situations they found themselves in. Maggie felt like she did not deserve a 'normal life', that it was 'too much to expect decent housing'. In a similar vein Tim knew that he:

> ... had come to the end of the road ... I didn't understand why, but I knew. I did what I could to make the best of it – better the devil you know.

Over time Maggie and Tim both reported that whenever relationships between boarding house residents exploded they would leave for a brief time. Tim's initial pattern was of short, sporadic spells sleeping rough, but these spells became more frequent the longer Tim remained homeless. Tim found that:

> Every couple of months things would flare up. It was easier to sometimes move out for a week or so until things settled down. I had a spot down by the river that no one knew about.

He also slept rough because the conditions in some boarding houses were atrocious:

> I was sick of living in lice- and rat-infested holes. In the last place I was bitten by bedbugs and you can still see the marks. It's easier to sleep out sometimes.

Sleeping rough is common but it is rarely permanent. Most people returned to stay in boarding houses because this was the only option they had.

CAREER DURATION – ONGOING EXCLUSION

The group on the mental health pathway has, on average, the longest homeless careers (mean duration 73 months) of the five groups. This finding is consistent with other studies that also report that people with mental health problems generally become entrenched in the homeless population[11-13].

Unlike other groups with long-term problems, interactions with other homeless people did not form the basis of routines. The routines of homeless people with mental health problems are shaped by the way people in the mainstream and other homeless people reject and exploit them. The social and economic context in which the actions of people with mental health problems occur, set up and maintain the preconditions for their ongoing exclusion.

People with mental health problems remain homeless for a long time despite the fact that they have few homeless friends and avoid many of the social practices that signal involvement in the homeless subculture. The social identification (acculturation) argument is that the longer people remain in the homeless population, the more likely they are to identify with other homeless people and homelessness as a way of life. This argument does not explain the experiences of this group. For people with mental health problems it is the way their vulnerability, isolation and insufficient incomes combine with the absence of family support and a dysfunctional housing market that works to keep them in the homeless population. And it is the way that individuals respond to and reproduce these conditions that is crucial in terms of understanding why the career trajectories of people on this pathway point in the direction they do.

MENTAL HEALTH PATHWAY

- The routines of homeless people with mental health problems are both constrained and enabled by the dual stigmas of mental illness and homelessness. People on this pathway respond to the actions of other people whose view of the mentally ill is often derogatory and laden with misconceived stereotypes. The people interviewed lived the experience of these dual stigmas by denying their problems and withdrawing from social contact.

- The experiences of homelessness that ultimately lead to this group's entrenchment in the homeless population reflected the different social structures that the group had to contend with and their different response to the homeless subculture and the stigma of being homeless. The social practices and patterns of interaction that lead to the entrenchment of this group in the homeless population were different from those of the people on the substance use pathway, yet the consequences were similar — both groups developed routines that emphasised their outsider status and, in so doing, reproduced the conditions that resulted in their becoming embedded in the homeless population.

- Most versions of the acculturation thesis emphasise that people remain homeless because they adapt to the homeless subculture. However, what the acculturation thesis has missed is that various homeless groups relate to the homeless subculture in different ways with different consequences. In the case of those entering on the mental health pathway, they are marginalised by the mainstream and by other homeless people. People on the mental health pathway remain homeless because there are few housing options and insufficient support to assist them out of the homeless population. It is also the case that the way they internalise and reproduce negative social attitudes towards the mentally ill structures their experience of homelessness. While people in this group did not identify with homelessness as a way of life, they did adapt to homelessness in their own way.

- Without a larger sample it is difficult to establish with any certainty whether the incidence of mental illness in the sample is typical of the broader homeless population. In both the literature and the public domain there are claims that a significant proportion of the homeless population have mental health problems[*]. There are a number of problems with these claims. First, they typically draw their samples from sites where the incidence of mental illness is likely to be high[14]. Second, what constitutes a mental health problem is problematic because different clinical and diagnostic tools produce different estimates. Nevertheless, in the context of the small sample size, plus a growing body of literature that challenges the representation of homelessness primarily in terms of mental illness, it is hard to escape the conclusion that the incidence of mental illness is generally overstated, particularly as an attribution of cause.

- The issue of temporal order further complicates matters. This chapter relates only to those six households who entered the homeless population with existing mental health problems. There were another 18 who reported that mental health problems arose after they became homeless. This means that those on the mental health pathway represent about one-quarter of all the people who reported problems with their mental health. Most people in the sample who reported mental health problems experienced these problems after they had been homeless, which raises questions about attributions of cause and the impact of homelessness.

[*] On 19 December 2004 the *Age* newspaper headlined a story with: '80 per cent of homeless have mental disorder'. This story then became the basis for subsequent articles in *The Age* and other media outlets. In a sense it became true.

4 EXPERIENCES ON THE DOMESTIC VIOLENCE AND HOUSING CRISIS PATHWAYS

You never get used to it. Predicting it doesn't matter. Nothing I can do; he has complete control. It's always fresh, always dreadful.

Roddy Doyle, *The Women Who Walked into Doors*.

When reporting on homelessness the Australian media typically draw on a combination of historical stereotypes, along with stereotypes based on more-visible groups such as people with mental health or substance use problems[1]. Many researchers are convinced that these groups are just the 'tip of the iceberg'[2] and that a large proportion of the homeless are actually hidden from public view. The bulk of the hidden homeless are families and most are headed by women. Their relative invisibility stems from the fact that they rarely sleep rough or provide visual cues to their housing status[3, 4].

The homeless experiences of the people on the domestic violence and housing crisis pathways provide another perspective on the way homelessness is lived, resisted and reproduced, and there are three specific reasons to consider these two groups together.

First, in chapter 1 it was noted that both groups, on average, had their first experience of homelessness in their early 30s. This is important as career duration is linked to the age that people first experience homelessness, with longer careers typically associated with a younger age[5].

Second, in both groups the majority of households were families. This is also important as it has been reported that families typically have short homeless careers[6-8]. Third, the demographic profiles of these two groups are similar and their biographies reveal many common experiences, such as histories of independent and stable housing and involvement in the labour market.

As for all people, the condition of the housing and labour markets plays a critical role in shaping the context in which people make their decisions. However, these individuals negotiate the stigma of homelessness, and how their response structures interactions with other people and their day-to-day routines, in distinct ways. This explains why the homeless careers of people on these two pathways are different from careers of those on the substance use and mental health pathways.

Although there were some differences in the initial experience of homelessness, both groups exhibit high levels of psychological distress and anxiety, as well as sharing an expectation that homelessness will be a temporary experience for them. Over time, as they encounter barriers in the housing and labour markets, most households run out of places to stay and many are forced into boarding houses or caravan parks. At this point the pressure on families is significant and their distress palpable. Nevertheless, both groups resist homelessness and we identify three critical issues around which their resistance is organised: concern for their children; a desire to reduce stress; and minimisation of the stigma of homelessness.

Individuals actively manage the stigma associated with homelessness in a way that structures distinct patterns of social interaction with other people, both homeless and housed. The dominant pattern is to pass as normal. In attempting to pass as normal, routines are reorganised to minimise involvement with other homeless people.

An element of passing involves explaining their housing problems as a form of 'bad luck', and this allows for the possibility of change, as well as providing a means of distinguishing themselves from other homeless people whose housing problems are understood to be a consequence of individual failings.

Movement from one pathway onto another is a process that typically occurs as a result of engaging with the homeless subculture. Economic structures play a critical role in these careers, but to understand why these careers take the direction they do it is important to understand the way that individual actors respond to and reproduce existing non-material structures such as stigma.

FAMILIES IN CRISIS

After Lee and John had been evicted for arrears, their three children came home from school and were confronted by all of the family's belongings in the street. Avoiding the gazes of their 'interested neighbours', John came close to breaking down:

> I tried to explain [to the children] what had happened, but couldn't.
> We told them we were going to stay at their auntie's for a while.

Even though people react in different ways to losing their homes, feelings of embarrassment and anxiety are common. This contrasts with the experience of people on the substance use pathway who moved from housed to homeless with relative ease. This also illustrates how the same 'critical situation' is lived in different ways by different groups of people.

Like the experience of many others, becoming homeless *was* a critical situation for Sandra. Sandra recalled how stressed she was and how her anxiety was exacerbated by the impact of homelessness on her children. She felt that people:

> ... simply don't know what it's like to have no idea where you're going to stay that night.

Similarly, Frank 'couldn't believe it had come to this'. It drove Lyn 'crazy' having nowhere to call home, and Sally felt that being homeless was to be 'intellectually branded ... a non-achiever in a society that values achievement'.

Although the two groups share many experiences, the initial experience of homelessness did vary. Women on the domestic violence pathway indicated earlier involvement with the homelessness service system. Domestic violence has received significant government and community attention in the last decade. There has been extensive community awareness programs, a raft of legislative changes and the establishment of formal links between government departments such as the police and domestic violence services. These developments are in response to concerns about the high incidence of family violence across the community[9, 10].

Ten of the 14 women on the domestic violence pathway received assistance from services within a month of leaving home. Some moved directly into refuges, while others, because of a shortage of places in refuges, were initially supported in hotels before moving into refuges, and then to transitional accommodation.

The remaining four domestic violence cases, and all 24 of the housing crisis households, either had little idea there were services to assist them, or were reluctant to use them. While nine of these households spent their first night in a car or hotel, 19 turned to family or friends.

Homeless families typically expect to resolve their problems quickly and staying with friends or family members is a common 'first step'[11].

As the difficulty of securing permanent accommodation became more apparent the expectation of a short experience of homelessness began to change. After two months of regular searching Lee and John 'couldn't find anything'. Overcrowded living conditions, combined with no foreseeable solution to their housing issues, created pressure on relationships between family members and friends, and in some cases relationships were strained to breaking point. Sandra had taken her children to stay at her brother's place rather than contacting a domestic violence service. As a result:

> ... there were six of us in a two bedroom house ... I tried to help out and stay out of the way but it's bloody hard with two kids.

The resources available to these households were limited and many of the people they drew on for support were on low incomes themselves. This meant that the support of families and friends dried up more rapidly than might have happened with a middle-class family. Sally recognised that 'there's only so much people can do'. Sandra's temporary accommodation with her brother was cut short because:

> ... he had his own problems to deal with and found it hard to cope with all of us.

Most homeless households move to avoid these stresses and, in the process of moving from place to place, some households put their belongings in storage. This increased the financial stress that they were experiencing. Other households who could not afford to do this lost many possessions as a result of their constant moving. This was particularly hard on families. Lee and John:

> ... moved about five times in three months – it was impossible to carry all of our stuff and we left it all over the place.

A lack of accommodation at the lower end of the housing market means that there is increased competition for accommodation and, with rejections common, people's experience of homelessness tends to be prolonged.

For those people with poor housing histories this was a real problem. Sally had:

… a debt from the [housing] commission from years ago, and [real estate] agents can be choosy … I'm a single parent and too big a risk.

With few, if any, housing options in the private market and long waiting lists to get into public housing, homeless households commonly stay in inappropriate accommodation such as boarding houses and caravan parks.

Sandra and her two children stayed with her brother for a while, and then with friends, before they 'ended up in a [caravan] park', while Sally found accommodation in a boarding house. There was considerable ambivalence about both forms of accommodation. Sally could not come to terms with boarding houses and hated the fact that:

The shower or bathing facilities were disgraceful – they were full of scum. I spent most of my time worrying about the twins.

Sally found it hard to contain her anger about the fact that she had been 'assisted' into a boarding house by a welfare agency. This is a common practice despite the fact that these places are recognised as unsuitable and particularly harmful for children[12].

Once they were in a boarding house or caravan park it was easy to get stuck. After three weeks Sally:

… wanted to get out but I couldn't afford anything let alone find something … they were charging me nearly $200 for a room with a wash basin.

After six weeks Sally was 'beside herself'. She was worried that she was going to lose her children to 'the department'* but she did not have enough money to 'get out' of the boarding house. Sally was stuck – no housing options, insufficient income and no social support.

Once households move into boarding houses or caravan parks, routines that connect them to specific people and places – the doctor, the shops, school, transport hubs and the minutiae of day-to-day life – rapidly atrophy.

Disconnected from their old routines, many found it difficult to maintain the informal social networks that define day-to-day life. There was, for instance, no one around to 'look after the kids', and individuals reported that they were deprived of the daily gossip and everyday social interactions that connect people to the ebb and flow of social life.

Nevertheless, there was resistance to any form of interaction with other boarding house or caravan park residents. This practice strongly contrasts with the social practices of people on the substance use pathway, and there are positive and negative outcomes attached to this.

Boarding houses are important sites where subcultural practices flourish. People who were homeless because of domestic violence or a housing crisis maintained their distance from the homeless subculture by resisting involvement with boarding house residents. This meant that many households remained in a form of stasis waiting for 'things to sort themselves out'. Unfortunately, 'things' commonly didn't sort themselves out

---

* The Department of Human Services (DHS).

and everything started to get worse. Frank's case is illustrative. For the first few months Frank was in a boarding house he kept going to his old doctor who was 'miles away'. Frank did this because he thought it would only be a short time before he was housed again. Nevertheless, the travel across town created problems for Frank because it was costly. This resulted in his visiting the doctor less regularly than was necessary. Frank's health worsened and five months after losing his flat, Frank, still homeless, ended up in hospital with a chronic chest infection.

THE IMPACT ON CHILDREN

Constant movement between family, friends, boarding houses and caravan parks is particularly disruptive for families with school-age children – sometimes new bus routes needed to be found, sometimes it was necessary to reschedule lifts with other parents and for everyone it required notifying the school of repeated changes of address. Dealing with these issues makes it difficult to conceal housing problems. When households are under extreme pressure, such seemingly mundane and simple tasks can exacerbate the stress they are already experiencing.

Temporary accommodation arrangements resulted in some families changing their children's schools. Changing schools was the ultimate disruption as it broke many social connections. Lyn had taken her daughter out of school to avoid being found by her violent ex-partner. Lyn said that she felt like:

> … the cards were stacked against us. Jade's school was miles from the refuge.

The negative consequences of violence at home and homelessness on the health, self-esteem and education of children is well documented[13, 14].

Also obvious in these biographies was how homelessness disrupted children's day-to-day lives. Lee and John's children could not 'bring their friends home', and every time they moved to a new address their children seemed to 'lose some schoolwork' and 'fall behind'. Many families reported that it made their children withdrawn and prone to problematic behaviour. There was also rising tension between family members. Lyn reported that her young daughter 'blamed me for everything that had gone wrong'.

Despite the uncertainty in their lives, some families managed to maintain their children's attendance at the same school. While this was strongly influenced by the proximity of their temporary accommodation to school, it was also underpinned by a determination to maintain a semblance of stability in their children's lives. For Lee and John school was:

> ... the only lifeline ... it is important that they finish their schooling so they don't have to go through this.

When Lee and John moved in with Lee's sisters (twice in less than three months) they had to drive an 80 km round trip twice a day to keep their children at the same school. They wanted to keep things as normal as possible for their children but the cost in fuel, and the wear and tear on their car, meant they could not maintain this for long.

Constraints in the housing and employment markets create acute pressures on all low-income households, both singles and families, but the consequences for some families were appalling. Most parents endured considerable deprivation to give their children the opportunity of a normal life. On occasion some went without food and all were denied 'luxuries' such as 'going out' or any other form of recreation. While most low-income households, especially those with children, struggle to get by[15–17], for homeless families the struggle to provide their children with social, financial and personal support is even greater.

Nevertheless, everyone reported a strong desire to get out of the homeless population. And, among the people on these two pathways, there appeared to be three interconnected factors that galvanised resistance to homelessness.

The first was a concern for children, and this was specific to families – dual or single parent. Sandra was totally focussed on 'getting things right for the kids'. Sandra was 'embarrassed as a parent'. She felt like she had:

> … let the kids down. I found it very difficult to talk to other parents for fear of them finding out. I felt very uncomfortable around them and avoided them when I could.

Similarly, given the deleterious impact of homelessness on their children, Lee and John were not proud of the way they had 'failed in their duty as parents':

> The kids at school gave our kids a hard time and other parents looked down on us.

Lyn shared their concerns when she made the point that she 'was a good parent, but things just weren't working out for me at that time'.

The second factor that structured their resistance to homelessness was the desire to reduce the stress caused by ongoing residential insecurity. Sally was prepared to 'look anywhere or do anything' for a place to live. However, trying to balance her family's needs in the context of substandard housing was difficult. No matter how strong Sally's determination to get out of homelessness, she had to deal with conditions at the lower end of the housing market. Sally ended up 'looking at places in the middle of nowhere' and most of them were 'dives'. Sally remembered that one place she 'looked at had exposed wires coming out of the wall. I mean, with the kids'. Similarly, Sandra looked at 'heaps' of flats and her view was that:

You wouldn't let a dog live in some of the places I saw.

The third factor was the stigma of homelessness. While some households had been vouchered into boarding houses or caravan parks by welfare agencies, most had tried to resolve their problems themselves. The reluctance to use services was grounded in prejudicial stereotypes of homeless people and people who use welfare services. This is not to imply that there was no use of government or non-government welfare agencies – everyone used material aid and welfare services at some stage. However, among the people in these two groups the values of independence and self-reliance structured daily life to such a degree that even when it was clear that assistance was necessary, for many, seeking help was an admission of failure. John summed it up succinctly when he stated that:

> I thought we'd be able to sort it out ourselves.

Faced with few housing options, insufficient income and ongoing homelessness, people who travelled on these two pathways started to use welfare and housing services more frequently.

TRANSITIONAL ACCOMMODATION

At the first interview the majority of people were in transitional accommodation (80 per cent), with the remainder in crisis facilities. For 61 per cent of the people on the domestic violence and housing crisis pathways this was their first time in transitional accommodation. This distinguishes them from the mental health, substance use and youth cluster where fewer than one in 20 people were staying in transitional accommodation for the first time.

Those who went to domestic violence services were, on balance, positive about the responsiveness of the system. In contrast, most people in the housing crisis group found the system to be confusing and irrational. Sally was astounded when the local housing office 'basically said I'd have to be on the streets before they'd help'. Others found assessment procedures to be demeaning and time consuming. Lee said that:

> You have to crawl around to all these services ... people don't realise how much effort it is to get help.

Others struggled with the implicit pathologising they encountered. Frank's contact with a local support service illustrates this:

> They couldn't help me because I didn't have enough problems. It's like you had to be a druggie to get help.

Later he commented that 'junkies get things on a silver platter'. Sandra called a number of places and was told:

> They were full. I was told my name was on a list and to ring back next week. So I did and they said ring back again in a week's time.

What people encounter is a system at full capacity and this means that agencies have to be selective about who they assist. For people in crisis, waiting lists often appear impersonal and irrational. The demand for transitional accommodation is high and many people miss out as a result.

The households in this sample were 'fortunate' to get transitional accommodation, although there was considerable variation in the length of time it took to get transitional accommodation (from o months to 7.5 months). Once in transitional accommodation having a 'stable base' was important in terms of recovering stability and establishing predictability. Having somewhere to stay enabled people to 'settle down' and to 'stop worrying' about their situation. As the anxiety of the previous months began to disappear people started to feel better about themselves. Sally used her place as a basis for a fresh start and she made the comment that 'you feel so much better about yourself when you have a place'. For homeless people, establishing stability is crucial. Transitional accommodation provided this point of stability.

When households were stably housed they could re-establish basic routines – children's schooling could be stabilised, the chaos of constant movement stopped and people began to feel more positive about the future. Lyn, like others, felt that she was 'moving forward, slowly'.

BAD LUCK

When people were asked about their housing, a common response was to define their problems in terms of external events and factors: a run of bad luck or a series of mishaps. John had lost his job 'through no fault of my own' while Sandra was not to know her partner would turn out to be 'a complete arsehole'.

Luck, particularly bad luck, has always featured prominently in homeless discourse. Homeless people have traditionally been described as 'down and out', which means to be down on your luck. When applied to the less fortunate, the notion of bad luck has its roots even further back in time. In medieval times bad luck distinguished the hopeless but well intentioned from the hopelessly corrupt, immoral, vagrant, criminal types. Luck became a way of distinguishing between the deserving and the undeserving poor[18, 19]. This 'timeless' distinction is central to the way people who experienced domestic violence and housing crisis explained their homelessness, although they commonly adapted the original distinction between deserving and undeserving to fit their circumstances.

The debate about bad luck and homelessness is generally constructed in a way that echoes the debate about structure and agency. For example, Tracy and Stoecker[20] explain bad luck as 'a characteristic of the homeless themselves'. This is an agency account. Others have explained bad luck as a 'reversal of fortunes'[21] or a form of 'structural victimisation'[22]. The idea of structural victimisation draws attention to the point that some people are vulnerable simply because of their position in the lower ranks of the income distribution scale and not necessarily because of certain personal characteristics. This is a structural account. To have no luck, to be down on your luck, to be unlucky, is something that everyone experiences, but the consequences of bad luck are tied to a person's social and economic position. While bad luck plays out at an individual level, the financial vulnerability it exposes is a structural factor and this is the central point made by a number of authors[23,24].

Luck was one point around which resistance to homelessness was organised. Using bad luck to account for their housing problems meant three things. First, it distinguished them from undeserving people – people who were homeless because they 'chose to be'; they were 'lazy', 'dirty' or 'crazy'; they drank too much or took too many drugs – who had made bad choices and were undeserving of any sympathy or assistance.

Second, it meant that the cause of their problems could be located outside of their direct control. Frank summed it up neatly when he said the reason he was still homeless after six months was that he couldn't find 'anything I can afford. If there was more housing I wouldn't be here'.

Third, it allowed for the possibility of change. All Lee and John needed was for a 'few things to go our way' while Frank expected his luck to 'turn at any moment'. These subtle but important strategies are at the core of these homeless careers.

DISTANCING

For people on the domestic violence and housing crisis pathways, being homeless was a departure from their self-conception. As a result of this, efforts were made to distance themselves from the homeless. The term distancing is used to emphasise the processes through which people actively put themselves, symbolically and physically, in a position that is in line with their self-conception. Distancing was grounded in prevailing cultural frames and by an expectation of returning to a 'normal life'. Although 'normality' was articulated in a number of ways – a job, a home, friends – a 'normal life' had symbolic and material significance, which countered any sense that they were different or in some way dysfunctional.

Few people saw any similarities between themselves and the homeless and, in some cases, people were openly hostile. Sandra described boarding house residents as 'weirdos and junkies'. Sandra was judgemental towards all homeless people, apparently blind to the contradiction that she was also enjoying the 'benefits' of transitional accommodation:

Look at this place. It's fully furnished, it's in a great location and it's cheap. There's no incentive for them to change when you can get a place like this.

Lee and John's thoughts, though less strident, echoed a similar theme:

When we first got this place I didn't know what to expect ... I was half expecting a bunch of deros to be sitting at the front door.

Differentiating between the deserving and the undeserving homeless perpetuates the view that some people are homeless because of their own shortcomings or because they choose to be. This replicates the broader 'them and us' stigma processes that underpin mainstream treatment of the homeless and other marginalised populations[25]. John implied as much when he said:

Things went bad for sure, but I didn't expect to end up here. It's not like we wanted to be here.

Treating 'other' homeless people as undeserving shifts the responsibility onto individuals and away from structural factors. This conservative reaction towards homeless people was rooted in prevailing cultural values and, by accepting these values and the practices that support them, these two groups contributed to the ongoing marginalisation of homeless people.

This conservative reaction is an important element in the reproduction of homelessness. The symbolic and material patterns of conduct that accompany this group's reactions to the homeless, while creating a distinction between their homelessness and other forms of homelessness, reproduced the very stigma that they were attempting to avoid. Take, for example, living in accommodation set up for homeless people. Tenancies of this sort can challenge self-conceptions tied to normalcy, independence and self-reliance, as well as emphasise a person's new devalued social identity. This could create tension that was evident in some interactions with the local community. When Sally moved into her 'new' place she said that:

> The neighbours keep their distance. Apparently this place has a history – I heard the last tenants were full on. I suppose they thought I'd be the same.

To Frank's dismay he encountered much the same:

> Everyone in the street knew the house was an emergency property. They put me in a box and no matter what I did I was just a loser in their eyes.

Their experiences show that stigma can structure social relations in ways that individuals find difficult to manage. In these instances, stigma was inscribed in the physical environment of transitional accommodation. The following section considers how these two groups responded to this.

MANAGING STIGMA – PASSING AS NORMAL

While substance users have to deal with the physical effects of using, there is little to visually distinguish people on the housing crisis and domestic violence pathways from the domiciled. With few visual cues, the main issues people who have experienced housing crisis and domestic violence face in managing their stigma is how they manage information about their situation.

People use a range of strategies to pass, but one strategy this group used was to develop 'disidentifiers'[26]. Disidentifiers are actions, behaviours or attitudes that signal 'normality', and for most it was stereotypical notions of the homeless that informed the disidentifiers they selected. Frank tried to stay well dressed because he saw the homeless as 'dirty and unkempt'. Similarly, Sandra made sure that her children were well presented because they had 'some pride in our appearance'. Sally planted flowers in the garden and painted some rooms because she wanted it to 'look like a normal house'. John looked for work every day because he wasn't going to sit on his arse all day 'like they do'. A common tendency in stigma research is to characterise people as passive victims of the stigmatised identity. The way this group actively manipulated their environment reminds us that people can and do 'artfully dodge or constructively challenge stigmatising processes'[27].

Many daily routines were organised around attempts to disguise or conceal their homelessness. For many women this followed on from attempts to conceal the physical violence they had experienced in their previous relationships. The motivation for passing as normal was to avoid being tainted by the stigma of homelessness – in the eyes of women who experienced domestic violence, to be homeless put you at the bottom of the social order.

People on the domestic violence and housing crisis pathways had little in common with the homeless. They had few, if any, homeless friends, and they knew few, if any, homeless people. This group distanced themselves from other homeless people. And, while they minimised contact with the homeless subculture, they also retained some contact with their domiciled friends. Both actions are important to explain why, in comparison with the experiences of people on the other pathways, the duration of homelessness was so different for people on these two pathways.

CAREER DURATION – DETACHMENT OR ENTRENCHMENT

Detachment from the homeless subculture reduces the likelihood of becoming entrenched in the homeless population. This is evident when observing the mean cumulative career duration of these two groups – for people who had experienced domestic violence and housing crisis it was seven months and nine months respectively. The duration of these careers was approximately one-tenth of the length of the mental health careers and about one-seventh of the length of the substance use careers.

Nevertheless, there were nine people from the domestic violence and housing crisis pathways who had been homeless for over 12 months. For two households, their prolonged experience of homelessness was a direct consequence of a tight housing market. Sally, who had been homeless for nearly 16 months, had tried everything to get another place and was at risk of being evicted from her transitional property because she could not secure affordable housing. After stabilising her life, Sally was tired of the endless search:

> I tried so many places and they just don't take single parents. I know my record is being held against me.

Sally's poor rental history, combined with her status as a single mother on welfare payments, meant that in a competition for scarce resources Sally always missed out. With the threat of eviction hanging over her head Sally was increasingly anxious once again – all her gains seemed to be for nothing. Sally's experience shows that structures such as the housing market influence the experience of homelessness, not just the processes leading into and out of homelessness.

The remaining seven cases were all single people. This means that of the nine households classified as long-term homeless, 78 per cent were single. In each case there was evidence suggesting that single people adapted their behaviour to the experience of homelessness in different ways than families did, and with different and often more damaging consequences.

MOVEMENT BETWEEN PATHWAYS

As some people adapt to homelessness they move from one pathway onto another. This movement occurs at different rates, although it generally reflects increased involvement with other homeless people. With the passage of time, single person households are more likely to reconstruct their identities around being homeless – through repeated encounters with the homeless they are more likely to accept the identity of a homeless person. As the group of single people in this study became involved in the homeless subculture the probability of becoming involved with drugs increased, as did the likelihood of becoming entrenched in the homeless population.

Movement between pathways highlights the fact that the five 'ideal' pathways are heuristic devices. While the level of movement among people on these two pathways is modest, it nevertheless shows how variables such as household type affect how people experience homelessness.

Apart from the small group who got involved with the homeless subculture, few households had problems other than domestic violence, poverty or both. A lack of affordable, appropriately located accommodation was the major structural factor driving career duration for these households. When domestic violence and poverty are the main problems it is possible to intervene successfully, but only if the appropriate resources are available.

DOMESTIC VIOLENCE AND HOUSING CRISIS PATHWAYS

- People who experience domestic violence and housing crisis display little affinity with the homeless. As a result of trying to maintain normality, few cognitive or behavioural adaptations emerge. Their actions and behaviour suggest that theories of acculturation are inadequate in terms of explaining the career trajectories of people on these two pathways.

- What structures the resistance of this group is the social identity attached to homelessness, and the way this stigmatised identity interacts with, and is informed by, their past experiences in the domiciled population. One way to gain a better appreciation of these homeless careers is to look at the way people manipulate their social environment and social interactions to pass as 'normal' members of the community, and the way this serves to preserve and protect their self-worth.

- Research has commonly focused on the negative consequences of stigma – stigmatised individuals have more difficulty gaining access to resources, their self-esteem and self-confidence diminishes and they regularly confront prejudice and discrimination[28, 29]. Furthermore, it is clear from looking at the way homelessness is experienced by many people that the stigma attached to homelessness does have many deleterious consequences. However, these two groups demonstrate that the 'deeply discrediting'[30] qualities of being homeless can be manipulated at a micro-level and can form the basis for reinclusion into a non-stigmatised position in society.

- The homeless careers of people who have experienced domestic violence or housing crisis can be differentiated on a number of levels, but it is the collective response of passing as normal and avoiding contact with other homeless people that provides a crucial insight into the reasons why these two groups have distinct career trajectories. A consequence of passing is that there are few behavioural or cognitive adaptations. This makes getting out less complicated than for those who become acculturated to homelessness. Nevertheless, unless the material structural conditions improve, no matter how effectively individuals manage non-material structures such as stigma, these households typically remain trapped at or below the poverty line. This means that they remain precariously positioned in relation to both the labour and housing markets and consequently remain vulnerable to further episodes of homelessness.

5 TRANSITION TO ADULT HOMELESSNESS

The progression of some young people from early homelessness to long-term alienation … is not difficult to understand.

Helen Sykes, *Youth Homelessness: Courage and Hope*

Youth homelessness has attracted significant public and policy attention since the late 1970s. Despite this, it remains deeply ingrained in the social landscape. In the sample of 103 in this research, there were 41 people who first experienced homelessness before they were 18 years of age. This was the largest of all the groups.

In Australia, the US and the UK some researchers have argued that young homeless people go through a series of biographical transitions if they remain in the homeless population[1-3]. These arguments centre on the idea that if young people become immersed in the homeless subculture they are likely to become acculturated to a homeless way of life. It fails, however, to explore the reasons why some young people identify with the homeless subculture when others do not. This point and the reasons why are explored further in this chapter.

Two different groups travelled on the youth pathway – dissenters and escapers – and each group responded to the 'same' critical disruption of becoming homeless in different ways. The role school plays in the careers of some young homeless people highlights its importance for enabling the dissenters to remain connected to the mainstream.

The social practices of the dissenters are built around avoiding other homeless people and attempting to pass as normal. In contrast, the escapers move into the homeless subculture quickly and, consequently, their 'new' routines are primarily reconstructed in the context of the homeless subculture. This can lead to a range of behavioural and cognitive adaptations. The different social practices of these two groups are reflected in the different amounts of time that they are homeless. The issue of movement between pathways is also explored.

AT THE START

According to Auerswald and Eyre (2002) the initial experience of homelessness is characterised by feelings of 'outsiderness' which includes an overpowering sense of loneliness and disorientation. This is similar to the idea of a critical disruption and both ideas capture the initial experiences of the dissenters.

Dissenters were naïve about homelessness and most were 'scared shitless'. Two dissenters reported that they had no idea what to do and with nowhere to go they slept rough, although this was an uncommon practice. The more common pattern, and one that has been identified in previous studies of youth homelessness[4, 5], was to couch surf, stay with relatives or go directly into emergency accommodation. Although Nan had left home on a number of occasions, when she made a break from home she admitted to being 'terrified' about what might happen to her – fears of violence and of becoming a street kid flashed through her mind. Nan stayed with relatives for a short period before she got into transitional accommodation.

When she was in transitional accommodation Nan said she felt 'on her own' and 'embarrassed' that she didn't have a 'real home'. The embarrassment was most acute for Nan when she was at school and what Nan feared most was being labelled a 'loser'.

The relationships that dissenters had with other young people were influenced by the stigma of homelessness. Dissenters typically 'kept it [their homelessness] quiet' or 'to themselves'. Nan 'kept quiet' because other students 'could be cruel if they knew you were homeless'. Keeping quiet is one form of passing and was a common practice amongst the dissenters. It also challenges the perception that among homeless young people homelessness is a valued social category. In 'keeping it quiet' dissenters' actions signal a departure from accounts that characterise young homeless people as leaving home on a whim – as willing and active in their own demise. These nine dissenters were forced out of home because of ongoing conflict with their parents and they became homeless because there was nowhere for them to go.

In contrast, escapers entered the homeless population with an already stigmatised identity. Escapers reported that from an early age they had felt discarded by their families and by society – they were from 'failed' or 'fucked up' families. This feeling of rejection was not passively accepted. In response to their exclusion from and rejection by the mainstream and their families, escapers openly recognised their 'outsiderness'. Escapers did not hide the fact that they were homeless. This is a clear point of departure between the dissenters and the escapers. Most escapers, like Robbie, 'didn't give a fuck who knows'. These different reactions signal an early, albeit tentative, acceptance of homelessness and this was central to the way the escapers attempted to make sense of their situation. For many escapers, having experienced what Auerswald and Eyre[6] describe as 'catastrophic family dynamics' for a significant part of their lives, homelessness could appear to be a 'better option'. In this sense the disruption associated with becoming homeless was much less for the escapers – in Andrew's case being homeless meant that he didn't have to 'worry about getting thrashed every night'.

WHERE DOES SCHOOL FIT IN?

A number of studies show that most homeless teenagers have their first experience of homelessness while they are still at school[7-9]. This was confirmed by the biographies of the dissenters and escapers but there were significant differences in the level of education obtained by each of these groups. This research shows that 78 per cent of the dissenters were in, or had completed, year 11 or above. Amongst the escapers only 15 per cent had progressed beyond year 10.

We also found that that the escapers first experienced homelessness at a younger age than did the dissenters (mean age first homeless: 16.9 for dissenters; 15.7 for escapers). This is consistent with other findings[10], which show that homeless people who report adverse childhood experiences typically have lower educational attainments than other homeless people, become homeless earlier and spend longer in the homeless population.

These findings are important in the context of Jon Smith's[11] study of 83 young homeless people. Smith makes the point that the age people leave school has a significant bearing on the homeless career trajectories of young people. He suggests that:

> Educational attainment affects young people's experiences of homelessness. In particular, it appears that the earlier young people left school, the longer they were likely to remain homeless[12].

School helped to provide the dissenters with stability and also an opportunity to 'get ahead'. School sustained their involvement with the mainstream and this operated as a buffer between the dissenters and other homeless people. This is important when trying to account for the different career trajectories of the dissenters and escapers.

Nan was lucky in many ways. Apart from a short period where she stayed with relatives, Nan was assisted directly into transitional accommodation. This happened because her school became aware of her problems at home at an early stage and when she was 'kicked out' they helped her to get assistance from a local agency.

In Australian policy debates there is considerable emphasis on providing early intervention to young people[13-17]. For most young people this means providing assistance early in their homeless careers by giving them the opportunity to address the problems at home while they remain at school. Where a return home is unlikely, then staying at school is considered an important goal in its own right. Early intervention works if schools are connected to early intervention services and have the wherewithal to assist young people who are experiencing troubles at home. It also requires young people to overcome their embarrassment and this is not always easy. Nan 'found it hard to talk about' her problems but she was fortunate to have a school friend who had been through a similar experience.

In contrast, the family life of escapers was characterised by chronic instability and trauma. This generally resulted in frequent disruptions to their schooling. Andrew recalled that he:

> ... moved housed all the time when I was growing up. I was in eight schools.

Although there was variation in the length of time between becoming homeless and leaving school, by the time escapers entered the homeless population, truancy was common and if assistance was not provided at this point, it did not take long before truancy gave way to withdrawal from school.

For escapers the withdrawal from school at an early age marked an important point in their homeless careers. Having no family support, and little education or work experience, escapers were more likely to be attracted to the homeless subculture because it mitigated their devalued social identities by providing a social space where they felt 'accepted'.

THE HOMELESS SUBCULTURE – AVOIDING IT, ENGAGING WITH IT

Dissenters

Dissenters had mixed views on homelessness. A small number stated that the freedom of homelessness was 'cool' and that they enjoyed being viewed as something of 'a rebel'. For most, however, mainstream norms prevailed and produced negative associations with a homeless identity. These norms implied that people are homeless because they chose to be, or because of individual failings such as drug or alcohol abuse. Expressing this perception of homelessness suggests that dissenters had internalised the values and beliefs of the dominant culture and in the process they reproduced the 'them and us' distinction.

The normative view created a certain amount of tension as people struggled with their 'housing problems'. Some felt embarrassed about their situation and adopted passing strategies that were similar to those employed by people on the domestic violence and housing crisis pathways. Nan's passing strategies were, for instance, built on a series of disidentifiers that perpetuated common stereotypes of the homeless. Nan stressed on a number of occasions how important it was to 'fit in', to be 'well dressed', 'on time' and to avoid talking about her situation in public so that others wouldn't find out.

School was an important institution for the dissenters as it defined their daily routines and social identity. School linked them to predictable routines that provided continuity and certainty in their lives. It was also linked to a specific social identity that countered, to a certain degree, the stigma of homelessness. For the dissenters, being a student remained the 'pivotal category' for their identity. Nan believed that being at school demonstrated that she was 'still a normal person' and this implicitly placed her higher in the social order. The dissenters also saw school as important to their future. In this way the dissenters showed their markedly different relationship to the future (or 'temporal orientation') compared with the escapers – two-thirds of the dissenters had thought about the housing they planned to move into when they left transitional accommodation. In contrast, 44 per cent of the escapers had thought about their exit housing arrangements.

While there is a distinction between escapers and dissenters, there is evidence that a small number of dissenters also 'enjoyed' the freedom of the street. A small group of three had 'slipped through the net' at school, as Chamberlain and Mackenzie[18] describe it, and began to engage with other homeless people. Over time they were drawn into the homeless subculture, and their lives began to resemble that of the escapers.

Escapers

For a number of reasons escapers received little assistance from their school. Many of the escapers were in their late 20s and early 30s and first became homeless before early intervention programs had started. Some were resistant to external assistance because they felt that they had already been 'fucked around' by people in the school system. For others, it had been a long time since they left school and they found it difficult to recall exactly what had happened to them at school.

Once escapers were out of school and in the homeless population there was little to do except hang around. Hanging around is a commonly reported behaviour among homeless young people[19]. It was a way for the escapers to meet other people in similar positions. According to Robbie it only took a short time before you were soon 'sucked' into 'the scene,' or the homeless subculture. Andrew said that he hung around the local shops and soon:

> ... started to recognise a few faces ... and mucked around with them.

Toni said that meeting other homeless young people was important as it provided basic information on how to get by. She met some people in the local 'pinnie [pinball] parlour' and:

> ... started to hang around with them – they knew about the services, where to get food, money.

As the escapers' experience of homelessness progressed, people started to share material resources such as cigarettes, food and information with other homeless people.

Friendships with other homeless people can help to dissipate concerns about being homeless. People spoke about 'looking after their own' and of people 'looking out for you'. The central theme was that homeless people could empathise with each other. Toni said that when she mixed with other homeless kids she 'felt better' knowing that there were others in a similar position.

The importance of other homeless people in validating their identity and their experiences was obvious. Rather than resisting the stigma of being homeless, Toni, Andrew and Robbie incorporated homelessness into their identity, creating a sense of purpose and belonging.

Social validation helped to make up for their rejection from mainstream institutions such as family, school and the housing and labour markets. However, to survive homelessness you needed to be street smart. The knowledge and social practices that constitute being street smart are an important aspect in the overall process of acculturation into the homeless subculture. This process starts early and some of the basic techniques and strategies that enabled them to survive homelessness were learnt during the initial period of couch surfing and hanging around. For instance, Robbie quickly learnt to 'carry as little as possible' and this meant he hid his few possessions where no one else could find them. It also meant that he carried as little identifying information on him as possible.

Use of the homelessness service system accelerated the process of becoming street smart. In youth refuges it was common to see the inexperienced mix with the experienced. Relationships between homeless people at different points in their homeless careers are one way that subcultural practices are reproduced. After spending time in juvenile justice facilities and a string of out-of-home care arrangements, Robbie thought refuges were a 'joke' because they were full 'of tossers who didn't know squat'. Hirst[20], Smith[21] and Mallett *et al.*[22] all make the point that youth refuges and night shelters are important sites for reproducing subcultural practices and knowledge. By facilitating interactions between homeless people, they are an essential part of transmitting the homeless subculture. Smith notes that:

> Life in services for homeless people and on the streets, where respondents met other homeless people, is an important part of the process whereby respondents both moved into a lifestyle and a culture of homelessness and picked up information needed to survive. This theme of companionship and learning the 'ropes' from other homeless people is repeated throughout the interviews[23].

Refuges were familiar to those who had been in juvenile justice or other forms of institutional care – the rules, the language and the attitudes they encountered, while not identical, were underpinned by a common thread of rejection and exclusion. Toni had been couch surfing for about three months before she got into a youth refuge where she:

> … learnt heaps. All the others had been homeless for a while and they sort of showed me the ropes.

In refuges, information about the 'rules' of basic social interaction was more important than information about how to get material resources. Toni quickly learnt that 'everyone gets sized up pretty quickly … you need a thick skin'. And a theme that emerged repeatedly was the need to 'watch ya back'. Robbie pointed out that:

Everyone is after what they can get and says anything to get it.

While Andrew said that:

You had to be careful … you look the wrong way at someone and it
can cause all sorts of grief and drama.

Interactions with other homeless people emphasised the
importance of looking after yourself. This helps to explain the
transitory nature of many friendships between homeless people.
On the one hand, friendships with other homeless people
provided important support and validation. On the other hand,
friends could turn on one another with, at times, surprising
viciousness and little warning.

The homeless experience of many escapers was characterised
by periodic use of the homelessness service system. Knowing
how to 'get in' was therefore important. The level of service
utilisation in the youth pathway was the highest (mean 5.5) in
the sample. The average number of times escapers had been
accommodated was 5.9. In contrast, the dissenters had been
accommodated, on average, 3.8 times. The homelessness service
system formed a key part in the lives of both groups but for
slightly different reasons and with different consequences.

The following section discusses some of the system
imperatives that also influence patterns of service usage, and
consequently the homeless experience of both dissenters and
escapers.

REFUGE ROUNDABOUT

Over the last decade or so welfare practices have been influenced by corporate notions of efficiency[24] and productivity[25]. Many critics have pointed out that these ideas are generally misplaced in the welfare context, but they continue nevertheless to influence policy development and program evaluation. In this context, 'throughput', or the number of people accommodated in one place over a specified period – generally a year – is used as a measure of efficiency.

Throughput is not inherently a bad measure, but factors beyond the control of agencies, such as the availability of affordable, secure housing, compromise its effectiveness as an indicator. Even worse, it can drive bad practice by motivating agencies to move people on before they have secured appropriate housing. Hirst's report *Forced Exit* (1989)[26] highlights that high throughput is pointless if people leave emergency accommodation to go into substandard accommodation or back into the homeless population. Hirst identified the way that young people who had been evicted or required to leave youth refuges before their issues had been addressed, would then find another refuge, and go through the same process. Hirst[27] termed the process the 'refuge roundabout'. The Burdekin Report[28] goes further, arguing that agencies that 'shuffle around people' are actively participating in creating 'chronic homelessness'. The interviews conducted for this research show that this practice still exists and is not uncommon.

The logic of using throughput as a performance measure appears to be based on the erroneous view that homelessness is typically a short-term crisis or 'emergency situation requiring an emergency solution'[29]. It is true that some households have relatively short experiences of homelessness and require minimal ongoing support. For others however the physical and psychological impact of being homeless, combined with problems securing a reasonable income, means that resolving homelessness takes time. This was the case for the escapers. Robbie spoke of being evicted and kicked out of 'numerous' refuges. In some instances young people acknowledged that their own behaviour was to blame. At other times young people reported that the practice in refuges failed to recognise the difficulty of resolving their problems. Robbie knew that his problems could not be solved 'in six fucking weeks' while Toni had 'heaps of shit to deal with' and she knew it 'wasn't going to be fixed up overnight'. This resulted in frustration, which was commonly directed at workers and 'the system'. Inadvertently, perhaps, the emphasis on throughput commonly compromised the restorative capacity of many of the agencies accommodating the people in our sample.

Street values

Frustration at system failures is one reason that people experiencing homelessness are known for exhibiting what gets politely called 'challenging behaviours'. Behaviours such as aggression, self-harm and harm to others (or threats of) can also result from other causes such as mental illness and substance use, though these states may well be a consequence of prolonged homelessness. There is a phenomenon known as 'service barring', where a person is denied service from a particular agency for a period of time due to their behaviour.

Even though the periodic use of the emergency accommodation continued throughout their homeless careers, 72 per cent of escapers reported that they had been barred from services. The escapers were almost twice as likely as the dissenters to have been barred from services (45 per cent). People on the youth, substance use and mental health pathways were nearly three times more likely to be banned from services than people on the domestic violence and housing crisis pathways.

The behaviours leading to barring can be understood as part of the homeless subculture. While not all homeless people adopt or develop such strategies, they are clearly a part of street survival, particularly once a person enters the boarding house environment. Many escapers started to rely on boarding houses because of the combination of reduced access to the homelessness service system, problems accessing housing because of their age, a lack of experience and a declining number of non-homeless friends who could provide temporary accommodation. If leaving school is the first critical point in the escapers' homeless careers, using boarding houses represents a second critical juncture. Toni remembered the first time she went to a boarding house as 'totally weird ... it was like you were stepping into another world'.

In boarding houses, young people mixed with residents who had adapted to homelessness and were more street smart. In order to gain acceptance from the older residents, young homeless people engaged in a range of social practices that were overtly antithetical to the mainstream. Some people 'took the piss' out of the rigidity of the 'normals' and their nine-to-five routines, while others emphasised the freedom offered by life on the street. Andrew mentioned that he liked:

> ... the freedom, the chance to do my own thing with no one around to hassle me.

Other respondents repeatedly emphasised the risks they took to gain acceptance among other homeless people and their expertise in managing these risks. Robbie mentioned an occasion where a group of his friends had 'pinched food and stuff' from a local supermarket. As they were leaving, the police arrived. Robbie said that:

> We fucked them right up (the cops) ... they chased us for about an hour, but we know how to get away.

Goffman[30] refers to this sort of behaviour as 'hostile bravado', a practice in which people try to outdo each other in a display of nonchalance about their stigmatised identity. In a similar vein, Anderson[31] argues that these sort of strategies, what he calls 'going for bad', allow disempowered kids to gain acceptance. Having been through 'the system', this sort of bravado was common among the escapers. It structured relationships among the escapers, between escapers and other homeless people and between escapers and the mainstream.

Early on in their homeless careers, however, with a limited understanding of the 'social structure' of the homeless subculture, 'bravado' could create problems. Andrew acknowledged this when he said, 'I thought I knew it all'. It was only after he was 'taken for a ride', quite literally as an unwilling lookout on an armed robbery, did he realise that he had a lot to learn, and that he was 'green'.

The aim of these social practices is to lessen the impact of stigma by giving people a sense of their own power. Unfortunately, by reinforcing the 'them and us' dichotomy between the homeless and the housed they help to reproduce the distinctions that stigmatise the homeless. Many of the social practices of the escapers produced similar contradictions. So while these practices enabled them to survive homelessness, they also interfered with people's attempts to get out of homelessness.

Although many of the social practices and meanings that make up the homeless subculture represent a rejection of mainstream practices, it is also the case that some are drawn from the mainstream. For instance, values such as independence and resourcefulness were held in high regard. However, these values were commonly manipulated to fit the social setting in which the people found themselves. Andrew told the story of how he:

> … heard [an agency] had money for white goods … three of us got fridges and sold 'em. Made a couple of hundred bucks out of that.

Cashing in the fridges was considered a great scam and there was substantial kudos for thinking it up and getting away with it.

The inversion of mainstream values was also evident in the way prison was incorporated into the homeless subculture hierarchy. In the homeless subculture, anyone who had 'done time' was virtually guaranteed a higher position. Robbie said:

> You'd hear that so-and-so had been in jail for rollin' someone or doing a job or something like that ... it was prestige like.

As escapers became immersed in the homeless subculture, their social networks began to change as they formed friendships with other homeless people. At the same time, they were becoming clearer about the rules and the hierarchies that structure the homeless subculture, as well as becoming equipped with a broader array of survival strategies. At this point many escapers reported that they identified with the homeless and that being homeless had started 'to become normal'.

'Using'

The use of drugs was one practice that was central to the process of acculturation and acceptance into the homeless subculture. Toni pointed out that other homeless people were 'not interested if you weren't using'. As Mallett *et al.*[32] and others[33–35] have found, drugs have a profound impact on the career trajectories of young homeless people, as with some other homeless people. The evidence of this study suggests that 'using' for those on the youth pathway was primarily a consequence either of homelessness itself, or of the underlying problems that ultimately led to homelessness (such as family violence).

Earlier it was pointed out that 10 of the escapers had had some experience with heroin before they were homeless. In four of these cases, young people identified a parent's or step-parent's drug use as a factor that contributed to their leaving home. For instance, Andrew's mother used heroin and he scored for her on a number of occasions. Where young people are exposed to parental substance use, Baron[36] found that this increases the risk that the young people will use themselves.

For the remaining six people, their involvement with drugs came via their experiences in state institutions. Robbie started to use in residential care where 'people shot up right in front of me'. Toni also blamed 'the department' for 'introducing me to smack'. In understanding the experience of this group, several points need to be made. First, most had typically only 'tasted' smack prior to becoming homeless – at most, they were casual users. Second, if there were no problems at home it is unlikely that Robbie and Toni would have been in the care of the Department of Human Services and consequently exposed to heroin. Third, their problems with drugs got worse once they were homeless. In comparison with those on the substance use pathway, it is clear that for this group substance use was a consequence of factors leading to homelessness rather than a cause.

In the broader youth pathway group, there were another 20 people who became involved with drugs only after they were homeless. The pressure to conform to the values of the homeless subculture can be seen in the different adaptive patterns of the escapers and the dissenters. Of the 30 people on the youth pathway who developed substance use problems after they became homeless, escapers were disproportionately represented with 85 per cent reporting that they had developed substance use problems. Given the backgrounds of the escapers and their involvement with the homeless subculture, a high rate was expected. In contrast, a third of the dissenters developed substance use problems. While still a concerning number of people, this shows that fewer dissenters adapted their behaviour compared to the escapers. While this can be linked to their different experiences leading to homelessness, it is also through the practice of distancing themselves from other homeless people that they avoided the normative pressures of the homeless subculture. Supporting this conclusion, the three dissenters who were 'sucked into' the homeless subculture all developed substance use problems, and their homeless careers resembled those of the escapers.

For most of these 30 people, involvement with drugs happened in the first six months of their being homeless. Researchers have noted that drugs are an important part of the 'process of initiation into street life'[37]. Many young people were surprised at how prevalent drugs were. Andrew, who smoked pot and 'drank a bit' before he was homeless, couldn't believe how common drugs were among homeless people:

> Everyone was into drugs – I mean everyone. That's all anyone talked about really – how to get drugs, what the gear was like, who had some.

Toni commented on how older people would target newcomers, offering them 'free gear to get 'em hooked'. Noting that the only time she received drugs for free was when she first started using, she said:

> [It] made me think the aim was to get me hooked ... I didn't think much about it at the time ... but looking back I can see how they sort of took advantage of me.

Similarly, a number of young people were introduced to drugs when they were in the homelessness service system. This confirms the findings of Mallett *et al.*[38] that some young homeless people are 'exposed to and started using harder drugs, such as heroin, while housed in refuges and/or supported accommodation.'

Using drugs immersed people in the homeless subculture, as can be seen in the three factors that characterised the biographies of young people who developed substance use problems. First, drugs were a way of dealing with the grind of homelessness. Robbie said that 'out there drugs is all you got ... drugs is your family, your friend'. However, if using was solely about coping then it would be reasonable to expect a more even distribution of problematic drug use across the sample. This was not the case.

Second, drugs were used as a means of self-discovery or enjoyment. Many people said that they liked 'the feeling'. The third aspect was the use of drugs as a means of dealing with traumatic life experiences such as abuse. The development of problematic drug use resulted from the interaction of one or all of these three factors within a social context where drug use was virtually a precondition of belonging.

While Neil and Fopp's[39] claim that peer pressure is not an issue among young homeless people who use drugs, this research found strong normative pressures to use in the homeless subculture. If you didn't use you were excluded from the scene and treated with some suspicion – an outsider among outsiders. This suggests that being part of the scene and belonging were significant influences on the actions of individual actors. Whether the catalyst for these adaptive behaviours was belonging, an act of resentment directed towards the mainstream or to cope with the daily demands of being homeless, using is a part of being homeless and for many young people it is hard to avoid.

Once they had started to use, it was clear that over time many began to use more frequently. Andrew spoke of how he and his friends would share food, smokes and information; they would talk about what was going on, who was new and who they hadn't seen, but mostly they talked about 'getting drugs and getting money to buy them'. Eventually Andrew's day-to-day routine was dominated by using and scoring.

When young people start using it commonly locks them into the homeless subculture[40] and they become focused on the here and now, as discussed in the chapter on the substance use pathway. Routines are directed towards scoring and the 'business of raising money' and getting out of homelessness becomes a secondary issue. When this happens their lives begin to resemble that of people on the substance use pathway and many make the transition to adult homelessness. Unless young people are assisted early, for many of them, homelessness is a pathway to substance use and consequently long-term, chronic homelessness.

HOMELESSNESS IS BAD FOR YOU

It is often forgotten that people's circumstances change when they are homeless. People who become homeless for one reason or another can develop additional problems as a result of their experiences while they are homeless. That people's homelessness can have different characteristics over time highlights the limits of the pathways concept, which needs to be stretched a little to reflect the complexity of people's experiences.

For example, the routines and social interactions of the 27 escapers and three dissenters who developed substance use problems after they became homeless soon resembled those of people on the substance use pathway. For people like Robbie, Toni and Andrew, using was an elemental part of their transition into the adult homeless population. Other changes had an equally significant impact on the homeless experience of young people. For 11 people on the youth pathway the emergence of mental health problems created new difficulties for them. Of these, nine also reported substance use problems as well.

Where both substance use and mental illness occurred, different responses to the stigma of homelessness, drug use and mental illness can be seen in the variability of their routines. People with dual problems moved back and forth between the homeless subculture and social isolation over considerable periods of time. In each situation there were different patterns of interaction with other people, both housed and homeless.

When people with dual problems are using they are typically part of the homeless subculture. When their mental health deteriorates, they are preyed upon and shunned in much the same way that people on the mental health pathways are. During these periods they tend to withdraw and become isolated. Robbie had witnessed many people 'burn out' and was sympathetic, but ultimately believed if they couldn't handle the drugs then that was 'their problem'. If we take reports of substance use and mental illness together, four-fifths* of the young people developed problems after they became homeless. Homelessness is bad for young people.

The phenomenon of changing circumstances is also particularly significant for illuminating the problem of temporal order, or whether mental health issues and substance use precede homelessness or are a consequence of it. The temporal sequence of events has largely been ignored by homelessness researchers and, as a result, the disproportionate representation of mental health issues and substance use in the homeless population has typically been cast in causal terms[41]. This study shows very clearly that the high representation of mental health issues and substance use can be partly explained by the impact of homelessness itself. Homelessness is bad for you.

When we examined people's mental health we saw how bad homelessness actually is. Although 23 per cent of the sample had mental health problems, two-thirds reported that they had developed mental health issues after they became homeless. While it is impossible to know whether these problems would have emerged anyway, people reported that the constant struggle

---

* There were 21 people who reported substance use issues only, two people who reported mental health issues only and nine people who reported both substance use and mental health issues.

to find somewhere to stay and a lack of security and predictability, combined with the stigma attached to homelessness, was damaging to their psychological wellbeing to the extent that they required hospitalisation. This over-representation of mental health problems reported in the homeless population occurs for two reasons.

First, irrespective of temporal order, if people have mental health problems when they are homeless they tend to be chronically marginalised by both the mainstream and other homeless people. With few cultural, social or economic resources they become trapped in the homeless population. Second, the data indicate that there is a significant risk of developing mental health problems after they become homeless, although this is typically mediated by drug use. This challenges the stereotype that commonly presents mental illness as a primary cause of homelessness. In this sample, most mental health problems emerged for people after they became homeless.

Substance use showed a similar pattern. Although 55 per cent of the sample reported that they had substance use problems, two-thirds also reported that they developed substance use problems after they had been homeless. This striking result has at least two explanations.

First, although substance use was a more common causal factor than mental illness in this sample, the data show that people who become involved in the homeless subculture are more likely to develop substance use problems. This is consistent with the view that people who come into contact with the homeless subculture are the group most at risk of developing new 'problems' such as substance use and this 'tends to perpetuate the problem of homelessness'[42].

Second, while substance use is a common problem, with over 55 per cent of the people we interviewed reporting that they have had problems with drug use, these problems were more commonly a consequence than a cause. Substance use locks people into the homeless population and, conversely, people without these problems typically exit earlier. As a result, this leads to a heavy concentration of people with substance use (and mental health) problems in the long-term population. The increasing visibility of this group has mistakenly been interpreted as the cause of their homelessness.

The extent of these changes can be seen more clearly when both issues are combined. At the onset of homelessness one-quarter of the sample reported either mental health or substance use problems. However, by the time of the first interview just under two-thirds of the sample reported that they had developed one or both of these problems.

Although temporal sequence is important on a number of levels, it must not be forgotten that regardless of when problems develop, the consequences are much the same – because getting out becomes difficult and the probability of a long homeless career increases. For young people in particular, this has consequences that continue to shape their biographies well into their adult lives.

LINKING DURATION AND IDENTITY

The adaptive patterns that emerged among homeless young people influenced the amount of time people were homeless. Among those who support the acculturation thesis, it is commonly argued that the longer a person is homeless the more likely they are to adapt their behaviour. The data suggest that the relationship between duration and identity is more complex, and that people's pathways into homelessness need to be considered as well.

Among the dissenters there was variation in the length of time they had been homeless. This research found that 44 per cent had been homeless for less than one year with 33 per cent being homeless for less than three months. There were five dissenters who had long-term problems – although two of the five had been in supported accommodation the entire time because they could not find affordable accommodation. The remaining three dissenters who had been homeless for over a year identified with other homeless people and accepted homelessness as an identity. Consequently, their experiences of homelessness were closer to that of the escapers than that of the other dissenters.

In contrast, all of the escapers had been homeless for over 12 months. Most had been homeless for many years. Some escapers were into their 30s and had been in and out of the homeless population on many occasions. This is consistent with other findings that have established an empirical connection between the presence of adverse childhood experiences and long homeless careers[43, 44].

For escapers like Andrew, the transition from youth to adult homelessness meant that by the time he was 26 he was embedded in the homeless subculture and homelessness had become 'normal' for him. Robbie, who had his first experience of homelessness when he was 14, was the most deeply embedded in the homeless subculture. With a sporadic employment and housing history and a long history of substance use, Robbie was still in the system at 37 and he made this point: '20 years later and I'm still here'.

THE YOUTH PATHWAY

- The different ways young homeless people respond to the stigma of homelessness and the homeless subculture impacts on the length of time they are homeless. The different responses to the stigma of homelessness show that stigma is not an individual attribute but a 'language of relationships'[45]. Young homeless people are not a homogeneous group and, while there are similar patterns of action and interaction, there is also variation.

- Young people's experience of homelessness can be characterised in two broad ways – some resist homelessness while others adapt to it. These different responses can be better understood by connecting them to the different sets of biographical experiences that young people bring with them. For the dissenters, their response to homelessness was typified by a resistance towards a homeless identity and other homeless people. This resistance was framed by stereotypical notions of the homeless as failures.

- For the dissenters, school was critical for creating a sense of belonging. Staying in school enabled people in this group to maintain and develop social relationships that connected them to the mainstream, which were an important influence on the actions and decisions of this group. School provided an effective buffer between the dissenters and other homeless young people. By remaining outside of the homeless subculture the dissenters were less likely to exhibit behavioural or cognitive changes that typically exacerbate homelessness. It was also clear that their familial experiences were less damaging than the experiences of the escapers. Consequently, the homeless careers of the dissenters were, in the main, much shorter compared to the escapers.

- Even though the dominant pattern among dissenters was to avoid the homeless subculture, there was evidence to show that some made the transition and had become involved with the homeless subculture. When this happens there is a tendency to become entrenched in the homeless population.

- The escapers initially perceived homelessness as a 'better' alternative than home. Many inverted the stigma of homelessness to provide a sense of belonging through connection to other homeless people; people consciously reflect on their social situation and are always actively engaged in making their own lives. Nevertheless, the inversion of stigma and the social practices that supported it came at a heavy price, which included chronic exclusion from the housing and labour markets.

- The much higher rate of adaptation among the escapers, particularly the high levels of substance use problems, suggests that early family experiences have a significant bearing on their homeless careers. Their lives show signs of being permeated by violence from within and outside the family. From a young age many experienced exclusion and rejection and this is one reason why escapers showed a stronger inclination to become involved with the homeless subculture where substance use was common.

- While the homeless subculture has positive benefits, identification with homelessness and engagement with the homeless subculture emphasises how social context and social networks can 'foster social learning and normative pressures that act as barriers to exits from homelessness'[46]. Further, as Auerswald and Eyre[47] note, 'the lives of the marginalised and homeless are not simply chaotic, but instead follow reproducible patterns'. Even though there are reproducible lines of conduct among the people on each pathway, the issue of movement between pathways draws attention to two important issues. First, it is important to delineate between subgroups such as escapers and dissenters in order to identify commonalities and differences that can enable more effective interventions [52]. Second, movement between pathways emphasises the fluidity of these social categories. This reinforces Fine's [125] point that categorical typologies can obscure complex social interaction. Pathways are ideal types that enable us to understand the world, but reality is always much more complex.

EXITING HOMELESSNESS

6 GETTING OUT AND STAYING OUT

And as Paul said these things to himself, a wave of sadness washed over ... He was understanding now that no man could live without roots – roots in a patch of desert, a red clay field, a mountain slope, a rocky coast, a city street. In black loam, in mud or sand or rock or asphalt or carpet, every man had his roots down deep – in home.

Kurt Vonnegut Jr, *Player Piano*

Information from the second round of interviews with 79 households shows that successfully getting out and staying out of homelessness has unique characteristics for people on each pathway. Four themes emerge from the interviews:

Housing affordability is a key factor for all groups.

The quality of the housing and its social accessibility contribute to people's staying out of homelessness.

Reintegration into mainstream (housed) society is as important as providing a physical dwelling. Successful strategies for reintegration vary by the person's pathway.

For people on three of the pathways, affordable housing is not enough to prevent further homelessness. Long-term, individually tailored support is essential for these people.

GETTING OUT – THE IMPORTANT ROLE OF HOUSING

What type of housing can be considered an exit from homelessness? And does it matter how long a person remains housed?

International studies on the role of housing consistently demonstrate that affordability decreases the recurrence of homelessness[1-5]. Appropriate, affordable housing is not simply shelter of any sort, as acknowledged by the cultural definition of homelessness adopted in this research. Homeless people often use boarding houses, emergency accommodation or friends' places as temporary accommodation, and these forms of shelter do not constitute getting out of homelessness. As previous chapters show, boarding houses and emergency accommodation are important sites of the homeless subculture and living there can in fact undermine people's attempts to get out and stay out.

What is the time frame for a housing outcome to be classified as a 'successful' exit? There is little agreement on this issue. This research shows that episodic homelessness is a common pattern. So how can it be determined if someone has really got out and stayed out, and is not just between episodes? Some researchers argue that 30 days is a sufficient time frame[6-9], others argue that six months is a useful measure[10, 11] while some argue that two years is an appropriate measure[12]. Whatever time frame is preferred, it is, to a certain degree, an arbitrary decision. Clearly, a longer time frame will better distinguish the processes that contribute to housing stability from those that contribute to continuing homelessness. This research used the observation period between the first and second interviews as the de facto time frame – a period of approximately nine months.

Affordable housing is important for people on all the pathways and underlines the big difference between finding accommodation and getting out and staying out of homelessness. To be effective in assisting people to get out and stay out, housing must be more than simply a roof over one's head. Housing type, quality, affordability and its social accessibility all play an essential role in people's housing stability.

One hundred and three households participated in the first round of interviews. At the time all were in transitional or crisis accommodation. Seventy-nine of these households were reinterviewed between nine and 12 months later. At the time of the second interview they had all left transitional accommodation. The following analysis focuses on these 79 households.

Seventy-two per cent were housed immediately after they left transitional accommodation. Most of this group (84 per cent) were living in public housing, and the remaining 16 per cent were living in private rental housing.

It is worth noting here that the high percentage of people who moved directly into public housing reflects the fact that transitional tenants are given priority access through a policy known as the segmented waiting list. This policy was designed to overcome the barriers that homeless people commonly encounter in the housing market by providing 'quicker' access to affordable housing.

Overall in Australia, the demand for public housing continually exceeds supply, and waiting times for public housing are notoriously long. This is the result of a small stock base combined with declining investment in real terms over the last fifteen years. In Australia the role of the state in the direct provision of housing is relatively minor. Social housing accounts for six per cent of the total housing stock, in comparison with England and France at just over 20 per cent, and the Netherlands and Sweden at 40 per cent[13, 14, *]. Furthermore, funding for social housing in Australia has declined, both in real and nominal terms, since 1991–1992. In the period between 1992–1993 and 2002–2003 funding declined by over 28 per cent[15]. This has contributed to an overall decline in public housing stock of 4.2 per cent since 1999–2000 (from 362,967 to 348,012 units), with stock levels in Victoria declining by 1.8 per cent (65,996 to 64,849) over the same period[16].

Did the type of housing affect the sustainability of these exits from homelessness? At the time of their second interview, 49 households (62 per cent) were still housed and just over 38 per cent were homeless. This means that over the nine-month period between interviews the number of households who were housed had declined by 10 per cent and the number who were homeless had increased by a corresponding amount.

Further analysis shows that social housing increased people's likelihood of staying housed. At the second interview, 90 per cent of the people who exited into social housing were still housed, compared to 67 per cent of those who went into private rental. These results confirm the findings discussed above that subsidised housing is an important factor in preventing the recurrence of homelessness.

---

* Australia's relatively low percentage of social housing is, however, higher than that in the US where approximately two per cent of housing stock is publicly owned or managed.

Despite this clear trend, five people who exited to public housing became homeless again. Affordable housing is always important but, for some people, even with the provision of affordable housing, staying out of homelessness was difficult. This research was able to enquire into the factors that made a difference.

Conversely, six households who had exited into private rental, and who were, on average, paying 39 per cent of their income on rent (as against 27 per cent among public renters) were still housed. This suggests that for some households, staying out of homelessness is not just about having affordable housing.

Did the pathway into homelessness affect people's housing stability? A clear, and by now familiar, pattern emerged when housing outcomes were considered for each of the five entry pathways. Table 6.1 shows that only 10 per cent of those on the domestic violence pathways and 21 per cent of those on the housing crisis pathways were homeless at the follow-up interview. In contrast, the number of households who remained or became homeless was much higher amongst individuals on the substance use (44 per cent), mental health (50 per cent) and youth pathways (50 per cent).

Table 6.1 Housing status by pathway at the second interview (per cent)

Housing status	Substance use (N=16)	Mental health (N=4)	Youth (N=30)	Domestic violence (N=10)	Housing crisis (N=19)	TOTAL (N=79)
Housed	56	50	50	90	79	62
Homeless	44	50	50	10	21	38
Total	**100**	**100**	**100**	**100**	**100**	**100**

Cluster one – housed
52 per cent

Cluster two – housed
83 per cent

As can be seen in Table 6.1, the data converge in the two clusters discussed previously. The people on the housing crisis and domestic violence pathways – cluster two – were more successful in getting out and staying out. The following section explains what made this group so successful.

STAYING OUT

Domestic violence and housing crisis
The experience of people on the domestic violence and housing crisis pathways showed two important themes. First, that affordable housing allowed people to reclaim their 'normality' by establishing routines and remaking social connections. Second, that housing location and quality played a role just as important as affordability. Affordable housing that is low quality and socially isolating can contribute to further experiences of housing breakdown. In both cases, the impact of a person's housing situation on their self-esteem is shown to be critical. How these households viewed themselves and how they thought others viewed them was linked to their housing status.

While affordable housing cannot on its own resolve a household's impoverishment[17, 18], it is also clear that housing provides people with an essential 'sense of personal efficacy'[19]. A sense of personal efficacy and self-worth was evident in a number of ways. For example, getting out of the homeless population improved Sandra's self-esteem – being housed meant that she no longer 'felt like a failure' and she felt more confident in her interactions with others. Sandra had 'put up pictures' in her home and was starting to 'invite friends around'.

Being housed located people physically and symbolically in the mainstream and this emphasised their 'normality'. Lee, who was on the housing crisis pathway, felt better now that she 'didn't have to pretend' everything was going well. As discussed in earlier chapters, becoming and being homeless for some individuals involved a radical departure from their normative ideals. These households consequently made considerable effort to manage 'their' social identity in ways that were congruent with their identity standard(s) and to do this they distanced themselves from the homeless as a 'general social category'[20]. This commonly took the form of passing – presenting themselves as non-homeless.

The strategy of passing highlights one of the ways in which the stigma of homelessness informs the process of getting out. People in the first cluster mobilised stigma in a slightly different and less successful way when trying to stay out. The strategy of distancing themselves from other homeless people by passing meant that the people on the domestic violence and housing crisis pathways were less likely to have developed any complicating problems such as substance use or mental health issues. They were also more likely to be able to maintain, or quickly re-establish, connections with previous social networks.

Housing gave these groups the opportunity to re-establish routines. Stable housing provided many simple yet essential amenities, often taken for granted by the housed, such as an address and a phone number. This was evident as people began to turn their attention to schooling, work and reconnecting to their social networks – that is, towards what they viewed as a normal life. Sandra spoke about how her family could now:

… plan things a bit better. I'm not always worrying about how we're going to get by.

John, from the housing crisis pathway, connected with his neighbour who shared his passion for fishing. For the first time 'in ages', John said, 'things feel almost back to normal'. In stable housing people could learn transport routes and times, recognise local shop keepers and get to know local residents. These may be small things, but they are the sort of mundane interactions that provide continuity, familiarity and predictability.

People also started to think about their future once they were established in their own housing. Lyn, who was on the domestic violence pathway, had been in public housing for nearly nine months and she wanted to 'progress to her own home' and start to 'move forward'. Lyn wanted to leave her housing problems behind her. Homelessness was a 'bad memory', one of those things that 'happen' and she did not want to dwell on it. Lyn, along with John, Lee and Sandra, aspired to a 'traditional' housing career – according to Lyn, to have your own home demonstrated that she was 'a normal person'.

For the majority of people on these two pathways affordable housing meant that they had greater success in getting out and staying out of the homeless population. These people had generally maintained some form of connection to the 'mainstream', and few had developed additional problems while they were homeless.

Nevertheless, while the provision of affordable housing is important, for some people new problems were created by either the standard of the accommodation (primarily in private rental) or the allocation of public housing properties in areas where they had few social networks. For example, Sally, who was on the housing crisis pathway, moved into a public housing property she described as a 'concrete dog box'. It was so small, she said, that her children could 'not fit their toys in'. The house was miles from where she had previously lived and a long way from the shops. Sally had no car and, without one, shopping and taking the twins to the doctor was difficult.

Frank's problem was that he was allocated a public housing unit in an area where he had no social networks. These units were for single people who had previously been transitional tenants. The amount of late-night activity concerned Frank, but his bigger problem was that he was 'on the wrong side of the city' and to see his family he regularly spent two hours on public transport. Even though Frank's place was affordable, without the close support of his family he was isolated and at risk of re-entering the homeless population. After six months things had worsened for Frank and he was living in a crisis facility when interviewed the second time. Frank's experience makes it clear that affordable housing alone is no guarantee that people will remain housed. Factors such as location and quality are equally important factors in people's attempts to get out and stay out.

Frank and Sally's difficulties were caused by the limited supply of, and access to, affordable housing. Those at the margins of the housing market are frequently forced to accept substandard or inappropriate accommodation, and when this happens they remain vulnerable to further episodes of homelessness. The housing market failure directly impacts on people's attempts to get out and stay out, indicating that without changes to the supply of affordable housing, or increases in their income, they are likely to get stuck on the outside of the housing market.

In Victoria, as in other jurisdictions, housing policy attempts to address the shortage of affordable housing by prioritising access to public housing. Unfortunately, however, the quality or location of the accommodation can compromise the goal of preventing the recurrence of homelessness. Furthermore, priority access does not improve the supply of affordable housing and consequently competition among low-income households remains intense. Some people always miss out, as reflected in the fact that not everyone from the sample on these two pathways was able to get out, let alone stay out. Some people became homeless again, while many single households moved onto other pathways as a result of their exposure to the homeless subculture.

In summary, the dominant experience of those on the domestic violence and housing crisis pathways indicates that if people retain some connection to the mainstream they are less likely to adapt behaviourally or cognitively to homelessness. This makes it easier to get out and stay out of the homeless population if they can find secure and affordable housing.

Dissenters
Among those individuals on the youth pathway, 50 per cent were housed at the second interview, but these people were not evenly distributed between the escapers and dissenters. A significant majority of dissenters (75 per cent) managed to get out and stay

out, while only 41 per cent of escapers were housed at the time of the second interview.

The experience of the dissenters showed that staying at school and staying connected to a domiciled community were crucial factors in enabling people to maintain their accommodation and stay out of homelessness. In her study of young homeless people, Susan Fitzpatrick[21] argues that if young people are to quickly and successfully get out of the homeless population, avoiding the homeless subculture is important. The benefits of early intervention are clear. Dissenters generally avoided most of the negative effects of homelessness reported among the escapers. Early intervention assisted the dissenters to stay connected to the broader community and it enabled them to focus on 'getting ahead'.

In Nan's words, 'getting ahead' broadly meant planning a future around school and a job. Nan had just enrolled in a hospitality course and was very excited about starting it. She was also hopeful that her problems with her parents would improve:

> About a month ago I contacted them [her parents] to let them know
> I was OK and that school was going well. They seemed pleased
> about my course. It was good talking to them.

The dissenters' desire to 'get ahead' was reflected in their relatively short experiences of homelessness and, as with many people on the domestic violence and housing crisis pathways, they were able to use the stigmatised status of homelessness as a catalyst for 'getting out'. This shows again how people actively construct their everyday reality and how different groups construct different 'realities' to deal with the stigma of homelessness.

While more dissenters had stayed out by the time of the second interview, it is important to recognise that nine of the escapers (41 per cent) also managed to maintain their housing in the period between the two interviews. It had not been easy for many of them and there were signs that some people were close to becoming homeless again. Andrew said that he felt lonely and unsure and he found that:

Every time I get a little something in the bank something happens. It's harder than I had imagined.

Andrew had been 'through the system' previously and had been housed twice before. On both occasions he had been evicted. This time Andrew had a 'great house' and good support and he commented that:

They seem pretty patient with me, I suppose. Anne (his worker) hangs in with me when I'm struggling.

Nevertheless, Andrew had few economic opportunities and this meant that it was a constant struggle to stay afloat. For Andrew, and others like him, it would take time before they could leave homelessness behind, even with a house and support. The experience of homelessness had raised questions for him about self-worth and social position that were not easily answered or quickly addressed. With the experience of homelessness still reasonably fresh in his mind – 'you don't just forget about it' – Andrew was worried about 'being drawn back into that lifestyle'. For Andrew, being an 'ex' still informed his life.

These examples reinforce the findings from the domestic violence and housing crisis pathways. While provision of affordable, appropriate housing is a critical element in getting out and staying out of homelessness, housing on its own is insufficient to ensure that every homeless person stays out of homelessness. While nine escapers had managed to stay out, the more common pattern among escapers was to have 'fallen over' or to have remained homeless throughout the observation period.

The experiences of all the groups who managed to get out and stay out confirms a strong and growing theme in the literature: that different homeless groups require different responses in order to resolve their homelessness[22–24]. The core argument is that some formerly homeless households require more than housing to stay out of the homeless population. This 'housing plus' approach emphasises the importance of providing different homeless groups with different types and levels of assistance to resolve both their material and personal needs. Homeless households commonly linked to a 'housing plus' approach include young people who have few independent living skills, people with substance use problems and people with mental health issues.

The 'housing plus' approach proves to be even more relevant for the groups who struggled to get out and stay out. This includes people on the mental health pathway, followed by the escapers and people on the substance use pathway. In understanding why most of the escapers had difficulty getting out and staying out it is important to recall that many had moved onto the substance use or mental health pathways, or both. Explaining the career trajectories of the escapers requires an awareness of how their attempts to get out were mediated by the lack of experience in the housing and labour markets, their adverse childhood experiences preceding homelessness, their connection to the homeless subculture and the use of drugs as a routinised social practice. The homeless careers of the escapers mirrored the substance use group, so the final section deals with the experiences of both groups.

STUCK ON THE OUTSIDE

The mental health pathway

For people with mental health problems the process of getting out of homelessness was difficult. They had long experiences of homelessness and, of the four people on this pathway who were reinterviewed, two of them were homeless again.

People cannot simply leave mental health problems behind them and this means that setbacks are common and overcoming homelessness can take a long time. Consequently, it is important that assistance is ongoing and that agencies are prepared to work with people during the good times as well as the bad. Maggie, who had been housed for six months, had a good ongoing relationship with her worker. Maggie liked the fact that:

> She [her worker] drops in and calls me every week. For once I don't feel like I'm on a conveyor belt.

More importantly, Maggie had been hospitalised twice in the period between the interviews and her housing had been maintained. For Maggie, knowing that her accommodation was safe meant that dealing with fluctuations in her health was now 'much easier'.

As already discussed, homeless people with mental health problems often lack family support. This often means that they require extensive 'external' support and assistance to reorganise their relationships and maintain the routines that connect them to the mainstream. This is consistent with the findings of Morrissey and Dennis[25] and Fischer[26] who all argue that adequate follow-up and support is critical in preventing the recurrence of homelessness among homeless people with mental health issues. Assistance also needs to be flexible and, according to Susser, Valencia, Conover, Felix, Tsai and Wyatt[27], support needs to be intensive at the start.

People on the mental health pathway had difficulties staying out of homelessness. The problem with helping people to stay out challenges social policy that frames welfare interventions around the ideas of 'self-reliance', 'self-sufficiency', 'independence' and 'full social and economic participation'[28-30]. These ideas, while laudable, are not always realistic as they ignore the long-term effects of homelessness and mental illness, and the complications they create for maintaining long-term housing stability.

Framing the resolution to homelessness in this way also misses the point that for a minority of homeless households, full social and economic participation is difficult given the social stigma attached to mental illness and the lack of resources dedicated to addressing the needs of the homeless mentally ill. Further, their fluctuating support needs make it difficult to participate in the labour market because the labour market is highly structured and routinised.

With good support, appropriate housing and realistic expectations, people with mental health problems can get out and stay out of homelessness. They will, however, always be vulnerable if they are not supported during periods of illness. This emphasises the point that people with mental health issues remain vulnerable even when they are in 'good housing'. And, unless community attitudes change, people with mental health problems will always be at the margins of society.

Escapers and substance users

The homeless experiences of the escapers and people on the substance use pathway were similar as both groups had been homeless for long periods of time and were deeply embedded in the homeless subculture.

A commonly reported finding about people with substance use problems is that they frequently relapse[31, 32], a pattern that was also evident in this research. Michelle, who had been in and out of the homeless population for over 10 years, said that:

> It's hard to resist – sometimes you lose the fight even though you don't wanna go back there.

The problem of relapsing indirectly draws attention to the fact that many people in the sample had exited homelessness on more than one occasion. Career models of homelessness, such as Chamberlain and Mackenzie's (1998)[33], tend to gloss over[*] movement in and out of homelessness, implying that homelessness is more or less a continuous experience. However, longitudinal studies of the homeless have consistently identified (and described in different ways) a pattern of repeated entry into and exit from homelessness extending, in some cases, over many years[34-40]. In this study, as in others[41-43], the term 'episodic homelessness' is used to describe this phenomenon.

A close inspection of the 79 housing biographies revealed that episodic homelessness was a frequent experience. Table 6.2 shows that 67 per cent of the sample reported that they had more than one episode of homelessness.

Table 6.2 Episodic homelessness by onset pathway (per cent)

Evidence of episodic homelessness	Substance use (N=16)	Mental health (N=4)	Youth (N=30)	Domestic violence (N=10)	Housing crisis (N=19)	TOTAL (N=79)
Yes	83	83	76	50	46	67

Cluster one
78 per cent

Cluster two
48 per cent

Following the by now familiar pattern, Table 6.2 shows that the higher levels of episodic homelessness were concentrated among individuals on three of the five pathways. Just over three-quarters of the people on the substance use, mental health and youth pathways reported that they had experienced more than

---

[*] There are exceptions. *See* Snow and Anderson (1993); Auerswald and Eyre (2002).

one episode of homelessness. In contrast, just under half of the people on the domestic violence (50 per cent) and housing crisis (46 per cent) pathways reported episodic homelessness.

While the problems leading to each homeless episode varied, they tended to reflect the interaction between the issues that led to the first experience of homelessness, and those that had emerged while people were homeless. Additionally, over time, episodes of homelessness tended to increase in duration, reflecting increasingly precarious relationships with the housing and labour markets, as well as an increasing acceptance of a homeless way of life. The level of episodic homelessness was more pronounced in the three groups with the longest careers and this suggests that staying out of homelessness is more difficult for people who have been involved in the homeless subculture.

Episodic homelessness presents something of a theoretical puzzle. If people identify more with homelessness over time, why do they keep trying to get out of homelessness? Sustained engagement with other homeless people creates routines that entrench people in the homeless subculture, and this typically results in identification with and adaptation to a homeless way of life. The acculturation thesis contends that the longer people are homeless, the more they become acculturated to a homeless way of life. Repeated attempts to get out would therefore appear to be at odds with the underlying premise of this idea, yet the data in Table 6.2 clearly show the continuing efforts of people to get out despite long-term homelessness.

Toni, on the youth pathway, made the point that, 'I only know homeless people when I'm homeless,' while Keith, on the substance use pathway, was 'careful to avoid them'. Not only had Keith 'distanced' himself physically, but he now described homeless people as 'them', rather than 'we' or 'I'. By recasting the homeless as the 'other', Keith was in the process of creating a new identity that distinguished him from the homeless, and from his past. These examples show that identities are constantly being negotiated and struggled over. And in particular that even after years of homelessness, normatively acceptable social identities still provided a clear point of reference for many. This reference assisted individuals to retain the capacity and desire to escape homelessness, despite experiencing chronic exclusion from the mainstream and finding support and meaning with other homeless people.

The prevalence of episodic homelessness highlights the apparent contradiction that even individuals who exhibit a strong identification with a homeless way of life also continue to resist homelessness. The tension between identification and resistance is reflected in the distancing strategies of those people who became involved with the homeless subculture and who typically had long homeless careers.

The following section discusses this tension in people from the substance use pathway and from the escapers group, both of whom were disproportionately represented among the long-term homeless. It shows that because of their strong association with other homeless people, their distancing practices are less successful than those of the people on the housing crisis and domestic violence pathways. For the escapers and the substance users, resistance to homelessness means breaking the link with their homeless peers and transforming their daily routines and habits. It is a formidable task reflected in people's struggle to get out and stay out.

Distancing strategies

In the process of engaging with other homeless people many people began to identify with a homeless way of life. Getting out and staying out of homelessness for people whose identity is linked to their experience of homelessness means more than simply changing their housing status – it means changing their social networks and reorientating their identity standards.

When people want to avoid the negative attention associated with a stigmatised identity, a common practice is to distance themselves from people who have that identity. People in the domestic violence and housing crisis pathways distanced themselves from the homeless as a 'general social category'[44]. In contrast, getting out of homelessness, for individuals who had engaged with the homeless subculture and who identified with other homeless people, involved physically and psychologically removing themselves from their existing social networks, which were comprised primarily of other homeless people. Snow and Anderson[45] term this practice 'associational distancing' and it involves people reshaping their social networks and breaking their routines. Establishing new social networks, breaking established routines, and re-establishing new ones is not straightforward for anybody, but there are a number of particular difficulties faced by the long-term homeless.

For the people in this study, associational distancing was revealed in the belief that to get a new life you had to leave the old one behind you, and to do that you had to 'leave the scene'. Keith was one of the substance use group who was still housed after leaving transitional accommodation. This was Keith's fourth attempt to get out. On previous occasions he had been 'sucked back to the action'. This time he attributed his success to 'removing myself from drug using environments'. Similarly, Andrew, who had 'picked up a habit' when he was homeless, said that if 'I hang around with them I'd be back on the drugs'.

However, distancing was not limited to 'steering clear' of other homeless people. Linked to the idea of associational distancing was the notion of 'being ready' to move on. This individual recognition indicated a desire to return to, or create, a 'normal life'. The idea of a normal life was not a fanciful construction. While the lifestyle of the long-term homeless stands very much outside the normative order, preferred identities tended to contain strong traces of that order.

Although many people spoke of 'being ready' this sentiment was stronger among people in their mid- to late 30s. At this stage in their lives many people had experienced over a decade of chronic housing instability. After long periods of homelessness many people expressed weariness with the whole scene – being homeless was too fluid and too contradictory to provide a meaningful sense of belonging. For those who had substance use issues, heroin had lost its allure, the physical ravages were pronounced and many had seen friends and acquaintances die from overdoses or other drug related causes. They had also witnessed and experienced a great deal of violence. Having endured years without stable accommodation, they were 'sick and tired' of the constant hustling and scamming necessary to survive. While the homeless subculture helps some people to regain or develop a sense of belonging and purpose, ultimately the practices that sustain the homeless subculture fail to provide the sort of predictability and continuity that underpin emotional and psychological security. Robbie explicitly recognised this when he said that the homeless subculture was:

> A front, a scene, a show that steals your life and gives you back a piece of shit.

For many of the older members on these two pathways the thought of returning to the streets filled them with horror. Michelle said that 'if it happens it will be the last time, I can't go down again – I'm nearly 40'. There was a distinct transformation as people became, in Michelle's words, 'tired of swimming against the tide'.

Among people over 30 on the substance use and youth pathways, many said that they wanted a 'simple life', and for many this represented a life without the grief and drama associated with the homeless subculture. Michelle wanted:

> … some peace and quiet. I couldn't take that shit any more. I want my neighbours to look out for me, not hate me.

The catalyst for Michelle was the death of a friend, and at 39 Michelle knew she 'had to clean up her act' otherwise she too would probably 'end up dead somewhere'.

For others the desire to get out was galvanised by the stigma of having their children removed. In this sense children frequently provided the impetus for getting out. Toni had been deeply embedded in the homeless subculture and she carried the emotional and physical scars of using and homelessness. By the second interview Toni had been continuously housed for the longest time in her life, and she was proud of the fact that her kids:

> ... had a roof over their heads and food in the cupboard. If I didn't have them (the children) I don't know where I'd be – probably back on the streets.

Parents are often motivated to 'get out' of homelessness by wanting to be with their children, yet there are significant barriers to achieving this goal. Many had been involved with various parts of the welfare system and found themselves under some form of surveillance. Toni had to submit weekly urine samples 'to prove I'm not using'. As a result Toni was constantly reminded of her past and this made it difficult to 'leave it behind'.

Creating distance from homeless peers and the past is not easy. While appropriate housing is pivotal to the development of new social networks and routines, social networks and routines do not just happen when housing is provided.

One of the problems faced by those who had been deeply immersed in the homeless subculture was that after they were out of the homeless population, few had friends in the mainstream and most battled boredom and social isolation. When people are isolated and bored the possibility of re-engaging with their homeless friends increases. This in turn increases the likelihood of becoming homeless again. As Rice *et al.*[46] argue, it is important that the influence of homeless peers is taken into account to prevent ongoing or recurring homelessness.

Toni's experiences illustrate the tension felt by many escapers. Toni had mixed feelings – on the one hand she was housed and safe yet, on the other hand, Toni was bored, frustrated and increasingly depressed. Toni felt trapped:

> I just want to do something else – I want to get out of here and meet other people. It all feels too familiar, and I feel trapped … what am I meant to do? This is all new to me.

It was not only isolation and boredom that contributed to the problem of staying housed. Another factor was embarrassment at seeing or hearing about old friends whose lives had followed a more traditional pathway. Walking around the local shopping centre one day Keith saw an old friend:

> I was shattered. I could barely afford the rent and he had kids, a car, the whole family work thing. I was really angry and jealous too, I suppose.

When Keith attempted to distance himself from the homeless subculture, he found it difficult to re-engage with the mainstream. Keith's situation illustrates the problems many long-term homeless people encounter when they try to get out and stay out. For many the problem was that their emergent routines, so important in terms of creating predictability, continuity and security, were not deeply rooted. Consequently, these 'new' routines were easy to disrupt, particularly in the early stages of the process of getting out of homelessness. For these people the change from homeless to housed can easily fail without ongoing support to assist them in the process of social inclusion.

Having little in the way of material and emotional support, it was easy to slip back into old ways. Sometimes all it took was a small disruption and old patterns of interaction re-emerged. When John was interviewed for the second time he was homeless again. He said that he had been doing well and had been on bipuramorphenine* for about four months after the first interview. One day his script ran out and when he went to get a new one, his doctor was away and there were problems sorting out a new script. He 'lost it' with the new doctor and scored soon after. From there he 'was back on the gear in no time'. In John's case the lack of continuity with his doctor upset an embryonic routine that had distanced him from the homeless subculture. Once back among the homeless population he was on 'familiar turf'. He re-engaged with his old social networks and soon his daily routine was, once again, focused on the 'business of raising money'.

John's experience also emphasises that housing on its own does not address the long-term effects of marginalisation or the effects of long-term substance use. Some people reported that they found it hard to reconcile their past with the fact that

---

* A drug treatment for heroin addiction, similar to methadone.

'life had gone by them' and, for others, the internalised image of being a 'homeless junkie' was hard to shake. These experiences are difficult to overcome and it takes time to build a future and leave the past behind.

During the second interview it became clear that a number of people who had exited homelessness had also put considerable energy into finding work but without success. The reason for this was generally attributed to their poor employment histories. Even when they were housed, their long-term exclusion from the labour market continued and this meant that without sufficient income people remained acutely vulnerable to any financial setback. It also meant that they did not have the opportunity to develop new social networks that can occur in the workplace. For some formerly homeless people, such as those with mental health issues, work is a less realistic short-term option given their life circumstances and the state of the labour market. For others it is an important strategy for staying out. These people however, commonly had to deal with conditions at the bottom end of the labour market, which were highly competitive and typically tied to low-paying casual work. People also had to deal with the way potential employers reacted to their work histories. Robbie described his work record as 'a friggin' black hole'. In a tight job market employers can be selective and generally do not look favourably on people who have long 'unexplained' breaks in their employment records.

Another theme that emerged in interviews with a number of the younger escapers, was their having little idea that a 'normal life' had its own stress and pressures. Normal life tended to be romanticised and there was an underlying sense that once they were housed life would be simple and easy. However for many, particularly those with little experience of independent housing, being housed brought new problems and new stresses, and some soon found that 'life is not all smooth sailing even for the unblemished'[47].

In Toni's second interview she said she was 'stoked' [happy] when she got a place. She also admitted, however, that living in her own home was 'harder than I expected, sometimes I feel like giving up but I don't want to go back down there'. Toni mentioned that 'no one had told' her what to expect or what she needed to do to maintain her housing. Not only did Toni have insufficient knowledge about what it took to maintain housing, she also lacked confidence. This meant that she 'didn't want people to know I was unsure'. Although Toni was still housed she remained vulnerable because 'she let things drift'.

Over time, as pressures mounted and boredom and isolation grew, some people reverted to their old social networks. Re-engaging with the homeless subculture generally resulted in people losing their accommodation. If they had re-engaged or remained engaged with the homeless subculture when they were in transitional accommodation, they rarely got out of homelessness.

This experience suggests that creating new social networks is essential for reducing vulnerability to further episodes of homelessness. A range of formal and informal assistance to do this is crucial if people have few connections with the mainstream.

For instance, in negotiating the transition from homeless drug user to 'ex addict', some people relied heavily on informal support from family while others required more structured approaches. Narcotics Anonymous gave John support, structure and a routine. For John, Narcotics Anonymous provided a new social network and this was important given that he had lost his previous social networks in the process of getting out. For Michelle, even though housing had made a difference to her life, a number of small things had also made a difference. At the second interview Michelle said that her life was considerably better than it had been 12 months ago. Not only was she housed, but Michelle also had new teeth and she no longer felt branded because of the way she looked:

> I don't feel like people stare at me any more. I feel like I can make it
> this time, I really do.

Michelle found that by removing the physical signs that she linked to her past, her self-esteem had improved and now she felt more confident about making new social connections. She was, however, taking everything:

> ... one step at a time. I ain't going to rush this. I've been here before
> and this time I'm out.

Michelle's abstinence and her stable housing meant that she no longer saw herself as a junkie or as homeless, but increasingly as a 'normal' person. It is at this point, and not beforehand, that attention can start to be directed towards other issues like education, training and employment.

For others, a simple thing like having a pet assisted in the development of new social networks and routines. Keith was given a dog and he liked the routine of walking with it and the companionship, but most of all he liked the fact that he:

> ... talked to other dogs' owners down the park. It felt good. I was just another dog owner to them.

Addressing the cumulative impact and stigma of homelessness requires a range of responses. Once stable housing has been provided, it is important to nurture connections with the mainstream. At the same time, it is important to acknowledge that creating these connections can take a great deal of time, effort and persistence. Assisting long-term homeless people to get out and stay out must take into account the physical and psychological impact of being homeless, as well as the problems that led to homelessness in the first place. John made the point that to work through the past and build a future you 'need a long-term worker who helps you get to your goals – not halfway there'.

From both a policy and a practice perspective, John's statement emphasises that people cannot simply be 'reinserted' into the mainstream. As shown by this discussion, without any connections to the 'real world', people were drawn back to the social environment where they had connections.

Many respondents reported that they had previously been assisted out of homelessness. The provision of housing was important but they had repeatedly 'fallen over' without assistance to address the impact of years of trauma, neglect and exclusion. With complex and, in many cases, traumatic histories, many people found that they had to 'unpack the past' before they could take control of their lives, rebuild their future and reintegrate themselves into the 'real world'.

The cumulative impact of a lifetime at the margins of society is significant and policy makers need to be sensitive to this. Similarly, it is important to recognise the difficulty of disengaging from the homeless subculture, which is, for many homeless people, their primary social network.

Finally, even unsuccessful attempts to get out highlight the resilience of homeless people. Even after being homeless for many years some people refused to give up and unconditionally accept homelessness. The continued attempts to get out of homelessness show that 'even the long-term homeless individuals cannot be written off definitively'[48].

Another obstacle to reintegration into the mainstream is, in Andrew's words, a past 'that you can't talk about or hide'. Once people were out of the homeless population, many recognised that the prejudice directed towards the homeless continued. This translated into an issue of whether to 'tell or not to tell'[49]. After being up front, Toni decided it was best not to tell anyone she had been homeless. She said:

> People don't need to know the past ... their attitude changes, changes from who I am to a scumbag. All for being up front and honest.

Keith did the same and his response emphasises how the stigma of homelessness is a basis on which many people organised their lives, even when they were no longer homeless. Keith didn't talk about his homelessness because:

> ... it puts it into people's heads that you must be a druggie or violent.

For people who have experienced homelessness, managing information about their homeless experiences remains an ongoing process. Yet, even after everything they had been through, strong links to mainstream normative structures remained – toned down to be sure, in need of nurturing certainly, but the connections were there and, importantly, they remained tenable. The key point is that many homeless people wanted out, but did not have the support or experience to know what was needed to stay out.

While the practice of distancing helps to illuminate how people with long-term problems resist homelessness, associational distancing highlights the question of how stable homeless identities are. More specifically, it indicates that homelessness is not a categorical identity, but a contextual, relational and transitional identity. This suggests that distancing practices can, if properly nurtured, facilitate stable long-term exits from homelessness no matter how chronically homeless people may appear to be.

It is also vital to recognise that associational distancing, in particular, is fraught with difficulties and unless there is something to 'fill the void' when people get out of homelessness the risk of re-entering the homeless population remains high.

Support workers and program managers need to be aware that relapse is common. Nevertheless, once people start the process of reintegration, and have some success, the resulting improvement in self-esteem and self-confidence can make a real and tangible difference to their lives.

These struggles with identity and social context suggest that, while it is never easy, given the right material and emotional support, everyone who experiences homelessness can get out and, importantly, stay out.

PATHWAYS OUT OF HOMELESSNESS

- To understand how homeless people get out and stay out it is important to think about their pathways into homelessness and their experiences in the homeless population. Different social practices arise that reflect the interaction of people's pre-homeless and homeless experiences with housing and labour markets, stigma and subculture. Those people who distance themselves from homelessness as 'a general social category' typically stay out. In contrast, those who engage with other homeless people have much greater difficulty getting out and staying out of homelessness.

- The approach of this study goes some way toward addressing limits in the current understanding of routes out of homelessness. Some argue that the defining characteristic of the homeless is that they need a home[50, 51], while others argue that homelessness is 'rarely just a housing problem'[52]. In the context of a more diverse homeless population, both responses are correct. This means that the central issue is determining which response is the best one for each homeless person.

- Explaining how people get out and stay out of homelessness involves thinking about the different needs of different groups, and how these needs and experiences are connected to different ways of managing the process of exiting homelessness. These findings show quite clearly that what helps one group does not necessarily assist another group.

- The data certainly indicate that everyone requires assistance to secure affordable, appropriate housing. It also showed that people who became homeless because of domestic violence or because of a housing crisis are less likely to require ongoing assistance from support services. This is not to say that they require no ongoing support but, rather, the extent and intensity of the support is in general less in comparison to the people on the other pathways. The practice of distancing in the form of passing distinguishes these households and is central to their higher success rate in staying housed. While there was variation, most were eager to move on and 'get on with their lives'.

- For others, intensive and ongoing support is generally needed to address their issues. That most of the people who require ongoing support were on the youth, mental health and substance use pathways reinforces the view that how people become homeless, and how they experience homelessness, is relevant to their pathway out of homelessness[53–55]. Even if their housing problems are resolved, they may still re-enter the homeless population at some future date. This can occur for two reasons. First, many behavioural and cognitive adaptations take time to address and it is important for agencies to persist. Second, most have peer networks made up of other homeless people and without changes to these networks it is difficult to keep people housed.

- It is essential to recognise that all formerly homeless people have a poor position in the housing market and this limits their opportunities. With insufficient income this makes it difficult for everyone to get out and for many this also makes staying out equally problematic. While low positions in the housing and labour markets make it difficult to get out and stay out, these are not the only structures that constrain the actions of homeless people. The role of stigma and social identification are also fundamental to understanding how people *get out and stay out*.

7 HOW WE SHOULD RESPOND

What has impressed us most about the homeless ... is their resourcefulness and resilience. Confronted with minimal resources, often stigmatized by the broader society, frequently harassed by community members and law enforcement officials ... they nonetheless continue to survive materially, develop friendships, however tenuous, with their street peers, and to carve out a sense of meaning and identity. To emphasise this is not to romanticize the homeless and their lives but simply to recognise the many ways they confront their often brutalising circumstances.

David Snow and Leon Anderson, *Down on their luck: A study of homeless street people*

Australia is a rich and vibrant society with a standard of living among the best in the world. The idea of homelessness is strikingly discordant with the image of Australia as a prosperous land, rich in opportunities. Yet more and more people are now getting stuck for longer periods in the homeless population[1].

This book has presented some of the human stories within these statistics. These stories, generally hidden from the public eye, tell of the constrained choices homeless people face, and the ordinary and familiar strategies they use to survive. The voices of Frank, Lee, Sally and John told of battles with the tough bottom end of the labour and housing markets. Tim and Maggie's stories showed that mental illness is as confusing and frightening for the person as it is for everyone around them. Their experience presents a challenge to the community to better support people through the vulnerable periods so they don't become homeless and increasingly isolated. Lyn and Sandra bravely left violent relationships and showed the benefit of a relatively well-functioning support system*, though there is a need for more public awareness to mitigate the damaging impact of stigma. Nan's story demonstrated that school-based early intervention can help avoid the worst consequences of family and cultural conflict. The voices of John, Michelle and Keith told of the ravages of drug addiction made worse by stigma and a destructive subculture formed in reaction to society's ostracism. Possibly the most painful stories were told through Toni, Andrew and Robbi who all fled abusive families, often into a damaging state care system, and first experienced homelessness before they were 18 and became stuck on the outside.

These human stories, distilled from the voices of 103 people, illustrate five distinct patterns within the homeless experience. These patterns are termed pathways because they emerge out of the relationship between becoming, being and exiting homelessness. While everyone's experience of homelessness is unique, the pathways analysis provides a new understanding of what a person is likely to face given their life history prior to homelessness.

In all cases the shortage of affordable housing for low-income households can both precipitate homelessness and then trap people in a world of expensive, poor quality temporary accommodation options.

---

* Functions well for those who get in; turn away rates show that many others are left out.

The length and impact of homelessness, as well as the successful strategies for getting out and staying out, can be better understood by examining where people have come from. Using the pathways idea to frame the analysis provides some clear directions on the types of services that will better assist homeless people. This final chapter presents these findings, and suggests some of the changes to social programs that are likely to improve Australia's response to homelessness.

BECOMING HOMELESS

The common factor for people across all the five pathways was that they had extremely limited housing options because of their low income. This is a crucial point: poverty is nearly always the common denominator among people experiencing homelessness. Homelessness is not a middle-class problem; it is typically concentrated among the urban and rural disadvantaged.

The state of the housing market is a critical factor in producing homelessness. If there was sufficient, affordable, appropriately located housing, homelessness would have a fundamentally different character. In Australia, housing affordability has never been worse. For many low-income households home ownership is no longer a realistic option and the private rental market is so competitive that those at the bottom commonly miss out. More low-income households than ever before are struggling to maintain a place in the housing market[2] and more people will tip over into the homeless population unless this situation changes.

While increasing the housing options for low-income households is an absolute necessity, this research has also identified the factors that must be addressed to prevent homelessness occurring along each of the pathways.

In the first chapter, these factors were identified by looking at the change in how people interact with their surroundings as they become homeless. People on the mental health pathway had to deal with exclusion from the housing and labour markets, complicated by negative community attitudes towards mental illness, and a lack of family support. People on the domestic violence pathway had to contend with changes to their family relationships caused by violence, and the stigma of living in a violent home. People on the housing crisis pathway had to deal principally with economic constraints, in particular low income and a lack of financial resources for emergencies. Individuals on the substance use pathway faced negative attitudes towards illicit substance use as well as the way their substance use reduced their options within the housing and labour markets.

Two distinct groups emerged within the youth pathway – dissenters and escapers. The dissenters became homeless because of conflict with internal family rules. This was often due to tension between the culture and values of their family and their emerging identities. The escapers experienced physical and sexual abuse at home and, in most cases, had involvement with the state care and protection system. There were three critical forces impacting on the escapers. First, traumatic or adverse childhood experiences influenced the way this group interacted with other people. Mistrust and suspicion made it difficult for them to form meaningful social relationships. Second, most left school early and this placed them at the bottom of the labour market. Third, the escapers had to live with the stigma of coming from a dysfunctional family.

BEING HOMELESS

Across the five entry pathways, three distinct trajectories stood out. The three trajectories, which lead to quite different pathways for getting out of homelessness, were formed by the way people's backgrounds provided them with different resources and tendencies once they became homeless.

Each of the three trajectories was characterised by a distinct pattern in the duration and nature of a person's homeless experience. In general, their pathway in meant that they had different ways of negotiating the two interrelated forces impacting on everyone's experience of homelessness: the stigma of homelessness and the homeless subculture. Stigma is shown in the negative stereotypes and judgements that the mainstream applies to homelessness and is tragically demonstrated in the way people experiencing homelessness themselves reject other people in the same situation. The stigma of homelessness, coupled with fierce competition for survival resources, including access to illegal drugs, generated a predatory homeless subculture. For those who do get stuck on the outside, the subculture provides a sense of belonging and essential survival knowledge, which is ultimately destructive.

The trajectory with the shortest and least damaging homeless experience was dominated by people who became homeless because of domestic violence or a housing crisis. People in this cluster behave in ways that emphasise their normality and disguise their homelessness – a strategy developed in order to avoid the shame associated with homelessness. The strategy of passing is available to the people in these groups because of their pathway into homelessness. Biographical details such as their maturity, living skills, education, childcare responsibility, social supports, employment and rental histories gave them the resources and motivation to try to pass as non-homeless persons.

Passing is a way to deal with the damaging effect of stigma by denying that it applies to oneself. It is a creative and resilient response to social marginalisation. Yet while passing, like the other forms of distancing seen across the pathways, tries to minimise the harm to self-esteem on an individual level, it simultaneously reinforces the very stigma it attempts to combat.

In addition, their lives tended to be relatively mainstream prior to homelessness, and by passing, people in these two groups actively resisted any association with other homeless people and displayed few, if any, behavioural and cognitive changes while they were homeless. Resisting involvement in the homeless subculture was a key factor in minimising the harmful impact of homelessness, although over time these impacts were unavoidable.

While people in this cluster overall had the shortest experience of homelessness, some, typically single people, remained in the homeless population for quite a long time. This was mainly because of constraints in the housing and labour markets. With time, passing became less viable and adaptations to the homeless subculture increased. These individuals then tended to get stuck on the outside. Shortages of affordable housing not only 'cause' homelessness, but are also a key barrier that prevents people from getting out of homelessness.

Another group in this cluster was the youth dissenters. Their pathway closely resembles the experiences of people on the domestic violence and housing crisis pathways. Many dissenters maintain a connection with mainstream society, often through school or their social networks. They typically distance themselves from 'the homeless' to avoid being linked to the stigma or devalued social identity attached to homelessness.

The second cluster was mainly composed of the youth escapers and people who entered the homeless population on the substance use pathway. This group generally became involved with other homeless people early in their homeless experience. As a result, the behaviour of many individuals changed to fit in with their new social circumstances. They commonly described themselves as 'homeless', associated with other homeless people, focused on the 'here and now', and regularly used the welfare service system. They were very mobile and, over time, many started to sleep rough. In contrast to the use of passing, people in this cluster actively inverted the social stigma and appropriated the negative identity to create a sense of belonging. In this process, subcultural practices like illegal substance use and 'raising money' were gradually normalised. People faced much greater challenges getting out of homelessness once these behaviours became routine and as a consequence their homelessness typically lasted for a number of years. The stories of John, Michelle and Keith showed how even those people most completely adapted to the norms and routines of the homeless subculture recognise and suffer from its exploitative, damaging character. Assisting people on this second trajectory presents more serious problems for policy makers and service providers.

The third distinct trajectory was composed predominantly of people on the mental health pathway. They were isolated from, and marginalised by, individuals in both conventional society and the homeless population. They were frequently exploited in the early stages of their homeless careers and most sought to avoid exploitation by withdrawing from social contact, which then increased their marginalisation. Homeless people with mental health problems actively distanced themselves from two stigmatised identities: being homeless and being mentally ill. Similar to passing, this strategy attempts to preserve self-esteem by refusing negative social associations, but the consequence was to reinforce their isolation. Withdrawal and denial frequently meant that people in this group did not get access to treatment for their mental health issues. This cluster of people reported the longest homeless experience in the sample.

These three patterns in people's experiences of being homeless corresponds with different ways of getting out of homelessness. There is one more finding from these stories of being homeless to emphasise: homelessness is bad for you.

While we have used the idea of 'pathways in' to help explain patterns in people's experiences of homelessness, the research also shows, for example, that the youth escapers' experience resembles that of people on the substance use pathway. For some people, the experience of being homeless generates further problems, which then complicate their efforts at re-establishing a home.

This phenomenon – 'movement between pathways' – illustrates an important distinction between the causes and the consequences of homelessness. Popular understandings of homelessness typically focus on substance use and mental health problems as a cause. In contrast the findings show that approximately two-thirds of the people in the sample who reported a mental health or a substance use problem developed these problems *after* they became homeless. This finding is important because people with mental health or substance use issues have much greater difficulty exiting homelessness than do others. It is because people get stuck on the outside that these problems dominate the long-term homeless population.[*]

Attention to the stories of being homeless reveals the resourcefulness of homeless and formerly homeless people in making the best of the constrained choices that characterise their situation. Homeless people rarely, if ever, passively accept their situation. They continue to struggle to get out and stay out of homelessness.

EXITING HOMELESSNESS

The shortage of affordable accommodation is commonly cited to explain why people get stuck on the outside. And certainly,

---

[*] Coupled with the relative high visibility of these groups, this has led some people to 'erroneously interpret' high prevalence of substance use or mental illness as causal factors. This is not always the case. (*See also* Culhane, D, S Metraux and S Raphael, 2000).

for all people, affordable housing is a prerequisite for exiting homelessness. Nevertheless, some homeless people stay out of homelessness while others do not because of their background and the experience of homelessness itself. Assisting people to get 'back on their feet' is a complicated process not only because of economic constraints.

There are two distinct and important strategies people use to get out and stay out of the homeless population. Both strategies are linked to the idea of distancing, but differentiated by the extent to which individuals become involved with other homeless people. Attempting to pass as normal was a common strategy among people on the domestic violence and housing crisis pathways. This reflects their refusal to engage with other homeless people. In contrast, 'associational' distancing, or the practice of avoiding homeless friends and acquaintances, was used by those individuals who had become entrenched in the homeless subculture and whose social networks were comprised of other homeless people.

Findings from the study indicate that for individuals who spent a long time in the homeless population, and had adapted their behaviour and identity to survive homelessness, the availability of affordable housing on its own was insufficient. Individuals who became entrenched in the homeless population are commonly caught in a double bind – their interaction with other homeless people provides a sense of belonging but it also creates new problems, which in turn make getting out and staying out more difficult. Getting out of homelessness becomes more difficult as subcultural behavioural norms become routine. For these individuals, assistance must be matched to the reality of their situation. Along with treatment for past trauma, addiction or mental illness, they may need help to develop new social networks to combat the isolation and boredom once they break with the homeless subculture. These challenges are significant, and the pace of recovery varies for each person. If formerly homeless people are to sustain housing, the duration and intensity of assistance should be determined by the diverse needs of homeless people, rather than arbitrary guidelines as is currently the case in Australia.

The idea of a 'normal' life informed the actions of many individuals in this sample. People tended to use the term as a metaphor to signify a more comfortable and less stigmatised life. While there will always be variation as to what constitutes 'normality'*, in its broadest sense homeless people are surrounded by 'normality' on a daily basis – they see people going to work, coming from and going 'home', going out with family or friends and going to school. While many social practices isolate homeless people from the world of the 'normals', normality was a key theme that underpinned the aspirations and hopes of many people in this sample. Among individuals on each of the five pathways, 'normality' was a crucial point around which their resistance to homelessness was organised, as well as providing the basis for their reinclusion in mainstream society.

No matter how long people have been homeless, they still try to get out and get a 'normal' life. Chronically homeless people do get out of homelessness on a relatively frequent basis, but many have

---

* For more discussion of the term 'normal', see Appendix B.

significant problems sustaining their housing once they are out. The pattern of repeated episodes of homelessness shows that the current way of assisting these people is not working. Our results confirm what other longitudinal studies have found: namely that people who engage with the homeless subculture, and adapt their behaviour and identity over time, tend to become 'chronically mired' in the homeless population*. The pathways analysis enabled the research to distinguish some distinct patterns in how and why different people adapt to homelessness. Importantly, these stories also reveal that despite this acculturation people rarely give up and accept their homelessness.

For everyone who is homeless, getting housed is becoming more difficult because problems in the lower end of the housing market create significant barriers. A result is that more people experience homelessness for longer and their problems commonly get worse. While the size of the homeless population remains important, the dynamic and differentiated patterning of homelessness must be taken into account when designing assistance programs.

PRACTICE AND POLICY IMPLICATIONS

The dynamic understanding of homelessness presented in this book offers some insights into a world often hidden or stereotyped by the community and the media. A number of possible responses in welfare practice and social policy are offered here for those concerned with assisting people experiencing homelessness.

---

* However, the transition to chronic homelessness is not a linear process as described by Chamberlain and MacKenzie (1998).

First, at the level of practice, the findings reinforce the importance of listening to homeless people, and connecting their past with their present circumstances. In particular, the practices of crisis, housing and support workers can be enriched by identifying those biographical factors that appear to have a strong influence on a person's experience of homelessness. These could include the age a person first experienced homelessness, their pathway into homelessness, whether they have been in any form of out-of-home care and whether they have experienced homelessness on more than one occasion. Linking these factors to the presenting issues would enable a stronger assessment to be undertaken of homeless people's current and future needs.

At the level of practice three other points stood out. The first is that funding bodies must accept the fact that getting people out of homelessness is often a lengthy and complex process. As Caton[3] correctly points out, homelessness is a 'recurring feature of life at the margins' for many, and unless there is the right mix of support and financial assistance it does not take much to tip some formerly homeless people over. Many formerly homeless people remain vulnerable because they are living at or below the poverty line once they find appropriate housing.

Second, due to a critical shortage of affordable and emergency housing the harsh reality is that most homeless people are referred to boarding houses by welfare agencies. Private boarding houses are places where violence, intimidation and drug use are common. Boarding houses are also sites where people encounter other homeless people. Homeless people relate to other homeless people in different ways but, for some individuals, going into a boarding house decreases the chance that they will quickly get out of homelessness. Governments and service providers have been grappling with this dilemma for over a decade yet insufficient funds have been allocated to properly address the issue *. When people are forced to accept inappropriate accommodation their situations usually get worse. Low standards also express and reinforce the stigma associated with homelessness. When the most vulnerable members of the community are 'helped' into the worst possible accommodation the question that must be asked is, 'what is going on here?'

Similarly, while shared refuge or transitional housing represents an effort to maximise limited resources, it frequently leads to the initiation of newly homeless people into the homeless subculture. Without condemning the very hard work done by most assistance agencies, it is essential to recognise and confront their role in contributing to an ultimately destructive homeless subculture. The stories of people's experience of homelessness show that some assistance policies and practices designed to address homelessness are inadvertently making it worse.

Third, what is known about stigma and the subculture also suggests that longer-term support and a stronger emphasis on social inclusion are needed to assist those people stuck in long-term homelessness. Agencies try hard in difficult circumstances to get people out of homelessness and they do provide many

---

* In October 2006 the *Age* newspaper ran a series of articles that graphically described the poor quality of many boarding houses in inner Melbourne. The ensuing reaction highlights the dilemma that housing services face. Former housing minister the Honourable Candy Broad said, that 'referral agencies should not be dealing with substandard providers' (*The Age*, 14 October 2006). The minister did not specify where homeless people should be sent when there is no emergency accommodation available.

people with assistance in securing accommodation. However, agencies have limited resources and generally cannot provide ongoing support. Without ongoing support, many formerly homeless people become isolated and bored and this can compromise their capacity to stay out of homelessness. Without a meaningful role to perform, or new social networks to engage with, people often return to their homeless networks for support. When this happens individuals are in danger of further episodes of homelessness. Breaking the cycle of homelessness is complex, but essential ingredients are ongoing support for those who need it, and an explicit focus on social re-integration.

At the level of policy, three points stand out. First, in Australia there has been considerable emphasis on early intervention and this has primarily been targeted at young people and families. The benefits of early intervention are commonly understood in one of two ways. For the political right, the driving imperative is 'reduced government intervention and expenditure'[4]. For the left, early intervention belongs to what Billis[5] calls the social conscience tradition. From this perspective, early intervention is premised as a strategy that maximises opportunities for a full and participatory social life. Irrespective of what political view is attached to early intervention, early intervention is ultimately predicated on the belief that homelessness is a process and, for some people, an immensely damaging one. For all of these reasons early intervention is an important strategy.

In Australia early intervention has focused on schools, and the benefits of working with young people at risk of homelessness are starting to become evident[6]. For dissenters, early intervention programs assisted them to retain their connections to the mainstream and avoid the homeless subculture. For young people in particular, avoiding the homeless subculture is critical if they are to get out and stay out of homelessness[7].

This study confirmed that young people who have experienced traumatic childhood experiences or have been involved with the state care and protection system (the escapers) were disproportionately represented among the long-term homeless. Policy makers must develop, and appropriately fund, better approaches to ensure that young people leaving care do not continue to 'graduate' into the homelessness service system[8]. Those who 'graduated' generally developed additional problems such as drug use and mental illness, and sometimes both. This made their situations difficult to resolve. Not only does increasing complexity result in greater demand on the homelessness service system, it adds to a cycle of marginalisation that is difficult to overcome. There also needs to be further reform of the state care and protection system to prevent the damage many young people experience when they are in the care of the state. Put simply, when young people are deprived of any form of social stability, security and constancy in the lives, the long-term consequences can be devastating.

The second policy point is that early intervention can also reduce the possibility of individuals developing additional problems. While the aim of most early intervention programs is to reduce homelessness, there are indirect benefits that occur as a result of avoiding the 'effects' of being homeless. Obviously, this includes a decrease in the level of substance use problems, as well as reducing the negative impact on people's self-esteem, confidence and their physical health. In many ways early intervention has benefits for a range of social welfare sectors, not just the homelessness service system.

Similarly, many people developed problems with their mental health after they had been homeless. Preventing their exposure to homelessness may well have reduced the possibility of these problems emerging. For some people who developed mental health issues these issues may well have occurred anyway but the nature of homelessness is likely to have increased the possibility. While there was variation in the intensity and type of mental health problems people reported, the crucial and obvious point is that homelessness can be a deeply damaging and depressing experience.

The third policy point also relates to the problem of 'keeping people housed'. The development of the Support Accommodation Assistance Program (SAAP) was based on the assumption that homelessness is typically a short-term crisis[9]. This may have been the case two decades ago when SAAP was first implemented, but it is no longer the case. For some households homelessness is a short experience but, for many others, years of homelessness shape their routines, their behaviour and their attitudes towards the mainstream. Most people in this study who had been homeless for over 12 months had problems getting out and also staying out. For SAAP to remain relevant to homeless people it must broaden its emphasis in recognition of the increasing numbers of people trapped in the homeless population whose needs are increasingly more 'complex'.

Most agencies focus their limited resources on getting accommodation for people, while knowing that even with affordable housing there is no guarantee that everyone will remain housed. Snow and Anderson[10] emphasise the point that progress to long-term homelessness is typically a non-linear, discontinuous process. Policy makers must address this reality in their program designs. People who have experienced long-term homelessness and have adapted to a homeless way of life, and those who have experienced abuse and trauma, need ongoing support to maintain their housing once they have got out of homelessness.

Finally, like many approaches in the UK and the US, the Victorian model is based on a continuum of responses from an initial crisis response (temporary accommodation), then longer-term 'transitional' accommodation with assistance provided to seek affordable housing. This model works for some homeless people, but not for everyone, particularly the chronically homeless who have generally been through the homelessness service system on a number of occasions. In the US, the dominance of this model is currently in question[11-14], and the findings of this study similarly challenge it. One of the most traumatic experiences homeless people speak about – the frequent moving and uprooting from their communities – is built into a system designed to assist them. Chronically homeless people need to be settled immediately so that they can start the long process of addressing other issues – these issues are hard to address when the fear of moving constantly hangs over their heads.

In Australia there has been considerable effort directed towards developing a better understanding of homelessness. Much of this effort is focused on developing more-detailed profiles of the homeless population. This information underpins an endless debate about who is most 'in need' and tends to emphasise issues of individual pathology or disability. Consequently the role of social structures and social settings in the creation and perpetuation of homelessness is obscured. Exploring the dynamics of homelessness gives a better appreciation of the reasons why homelessness is very difficult to resolve for some people, and less so for others. This can provide a basis for better interventions to suit the unique challenges faced on the different pathways into and through homelessness.

FINAL NOTE

Homelessness is a tough, humiliating experience. Everyday, homeless people experience discrimination and the threat or reality of violence. They often wake up not knowing where they will sleep that night, whether they are going to get a meal and how they will stay safe. This research has shown why people respond differently to these issues, and what that means for the impact and duration of homelessness. Policy makers and welfare agencies can use this understanding to provide better assistance to homeless people.

In a country as rich as Australia, it is a disgrace that anyone should be homeless, let alone the tens of thousands of people who, on a nightly basis, are forced to endure the most demeaning and brutal circumstances.

Although homelessness is a complex phenomenon, its solutions are not. But, until the community can foster the political will to address the structural constraints that contribute to homelessness, politicians will continue to promote short-term responses and the number of homeless people will simply continue rise. It will be a national tragedy if we let the situation get worse when we know what needs to be done. Australians have the capacity to end homelessness. What is needed is the political leadership to achieve this vision.

APPENDIX A

RESEARCH DESIGN: TRACKING PEOPLE OVER TIME

Longitudinal studies that track people over time help to distinguish between cause and effect, and they also help to reveal the processes and strategies people use to get out and stay out of homelessness.

In this study two rounds of semi-structured interviews were undertaken. In the first round, 103 homeless households across Victoria were interviewed over a three-month period commencing in February 2003. People were recruited from five homelessness assistance agencies spread across Victoria, with two agencies in the inner city, one in suburban Melbourne (Dandenong), one in a regional city (Geelong) and one in country Victoria (Leongatha). Contrary to expectations, the research found no evidence of significant geographic differences. Approximately one year later, 79 of these households were reinterviewed.

Investigating the relationship between becoming, being and exiting homelessness required the research strategy to look backwards, assess the present and look forward, and therefore included both retrospective and prospective elements.

People's recollection of their personal history was used to bring out the dynamics of the relationship between becoming and being homeless. The first interview asked questions about the person's housing history to create a unique housing biography. Interviews lasted between 45 minutes and two hours. The second interview occurred nine to twelve months after the first and enabled a prospective research approach, including additional questions to elicit in-depth information about people's experiences since leaving transitional accommodation, and to cross-check material elicited in the first interview.

However, tracking homeless people over time is a difficult task and it raises the problem of losing people along the way. The study achieved a relatively low attrition rate (21 per cent) compared to other similar studies[1-3]. As stated, 79 respondents were successfully reinterviewed, while three people died before the second interview. Little difference was found between the attrition group and those that remained involved with the study.

This study is one of the first Australian contributions to this growing body of evidence, and provides unique data about homelessness in Australia.

DEFINING HOMELESSNESS

Definitions of homelessness are generally highly contested and there has been considerable debate in Australia and overseas[4-8]. This research uses the cultural definition of homelessness based on the arguments put forward by Chamberlain and Mackenzie[9]. It is best known as the definition used by the Australian Bureau of Statistics (ABS) to enumerate the homeless population.

The cultural definition identifies three segments in the homeless population. They are:

1. Primary homelessness – people without conventional accommodation living in the streets, in deserted buildings, in railway carriages, under bridges, in parks and so on;
2. Secondary homelessness – people moving between various forms of temporary shelter including friends' homes, emergency accommodation, refuges, hostels and boarding houses;
3. Tertiary homelessness – people living permanently in single rooms in private boarding houses without their own bathroom or kitchen and without security of tenure.

The cultural definition provides a practical, explicit framework for classifying people as housed or homeless at a given time.

APPENDIX B

Key theoretical and conceptual ideas that underpin the study

EXPLAINING HOMELESSNESS – INDIVIDUAL OR SOCIETY?

People make their own history, but they are constrained by the way power is exercised in societies. Men and women are actively engaged in making their own lives and consciously reflect upon events and social processes. They do so within material and non-material structures that both constrain and enable their actions. The variation in the homeless experience shows that what happens to people who are socially and economically disadvantaged is not predetermined. Families negotiate unemployment and poverty in different ways; teenagers and parents negotiate conflict in diverse ways; and people respond to housing problems in different ways.

Clearly, problems in the housing and labour markets are significant factors, but the findings warn against simple economic or structural explanations. It is not accurate to say that economic structures on their own determine the processes through which people become and remain homeless – these structures are important but their impact is mediated through other structures and the way different individuals respond to them.

Australian studies of homelessness have rested largely on structural explanations. The contention of such studies is that the major causes of homelessness are to be found at the 'level of societal structures' whose impact and effects extend across individuals and across time. Five structural factors commonly linked to homelessness are poverty, housing and labour market conditions, deinstitutionalisation and increasing rates of family dissolution[10-15]. While usefully describing the social context in which homelessness occurs, structural explanations can fail to explain why, among people who share similar social and economic positions, some people become homeless and others do not.

A second weakness with purely structural accounts is that they often treat structures as independent of human action, and as purely constraining. For example, in Australia researchers have generally focused on structures that have a material or physical aspect to them. The focus on housing and labour markets, rates of household dissolution and poverty reflects a tendency to treat structures as something physical or independent of human action. However, a housing market is not a 'physical thing' and although it has a material reality, it is comprised of relationships that are mediated or structured by the availability of resources, and through different legal and financial rules.

The focus on material structures has de-emphasised the role of other structures such as stigma, which takes the form of negative community attitudes towards the homeless, the mentally ill and people who use illicit substances. The role of 'non-material structures', discussed in more detail in the following section, was clearly crucial to the way people interviewed for this study negotiated the process of becoming and being homeless.

In contrast to structural explanations, there are also individual explanations that focus on homelessness. These are generally predicated on a belief that homelessness is 'reducible to the force of innate or acquired personal deficits'[16]. Individual explanations focus understanding and practice onto reforming individuals as the way to ameliorate social problems. Individual explanations commonly ignore the context in which people's problems occur, which can result in the overpathologising of homeless people. There is a danger also of shifting responsibility from the state to provide for basic human needs, onto the individual to reform their supposed character flaws.

This study set out to reflect the complex lived experience of homelessness by focusing on the interaction between structural and personal factors. Not only does this approach highlight that at the individual level structures are contested and changed, accepted and reproduced, but it also shows the way that people respond to these structures depends on, among other things, people's biographical experiences preceding homelessness – how they first became homeless, the social identity they attached to homelessness and how long they had been homeless for.

Use of the pathways idea shows that material and non-material structures are 'lived' in different ways. This point emphasises the creativity and activity among homeless and formerly homeless people, and shows that homeless people rarely, if ever, passively accept their situation. Studies that use the pathways concept generally recognise that the social practices that characterise becoming, being and exiting homelessness have both an agency and structural dimension. By examining changes in social relationships and social practices, the pathways approach provides a means of illuminating 'not just the relative importance of biographic and structural factors, but also their interaction'[17]. Although homelessness studies do this with varying degrees of success, the point is that the link between structure and agency is uppermost in the minds of researchers who use the pathways approach.

Nevertheless, the pathways idea cannot explain everything. Pathways are best thought of as a heuristic device that can help to organise complex realities. It is important to remain sensitive to this issue. If the pathways idea is applied too rigidly it can be overly deterministic, a point made evident in the form of movement between pathways. This movement draws attention to the fact that within each pathway there was variation in the way people responded to homelessness.

NON-MATERIAL STRUCTURES

The experiences of people on each of the five pathways reflect particular combinations and interactions of the material and non-material structures identified in Table A1, which in turn produce some typical patterns in the ways that individuals negotiate the experience of homelessness. Yet the findings also challenge the view that people adapt their behaviour simply to cope with the day-to-day contingencies of homelessness[18]. There is little doubt that coping with the stigma of homelessness and dealing with the daily struggle to secure material needs influences people's behaviour. The pathways analysis revealed clear variation in the way individuals responded to the contingencies of homelessness.

Table A1 Material and non-material social structures

Material structures	Non-material structures
Housing market conditions	Adverse childhood experiences
Labour market conditions	Family support
Poverty	Homeless subculture
Deinstitutionalisation	Stigma
Homelessness service system	

Because they are hard to 'see', non-material structures are commonly ignored as social structures by homelessness researchers, an interpretation that minimises the importance of these structures. This research highlights the impact of four distinct non-material structures.

The first non-material structure is termed adverse childhood experiences. Adverse childhood experiences include physical and sexual abuse as a young person (under 16) and experiences in the state care and protection system.

The second non-material structure is family support. A lack of family support has been identified in many studies of homelessness as a significant risk factor. In addition, changes in the level and type of family support can influence the way individuals interact with other social structures. For example, a person with a mental illness may be able to maintain their access to private rental with family assistance to meet their rental obligations when they are unwell.

The third non-material structure is the homeless subculture and the fourth is stigma. These final two are critical structures that all people in the study encounter, and the following section outlines this study's operational approach to stigma and the homeless subculture.

Stigma

For people facing or experiencing homelessness, the devalued identity attached to homelessness is as real as the shortages in the supply of affordable housing.

Homelessness is a stigmatised identity in Australian society, as it is in most western countries[19-22]. People's reactions can range from disgust to pity, but both indicate the negative social meaning given to homelessness. As a consequence, people experiencing the material deprivation of homelessness also have to negotiate the force of stigma.

Stigma impacts on a person's self-image and self-esteem, and creates discrimination in the housing and labour markets. Making things worse, domestic violence, illicit substance use, mental illness, involvement with child protection and poverty all have their own stigma, which shape the experiences of people on different pathways, and produce very different kinds of responses.

Stigma structures social relations and influences people's daily activities. When people become homeless, homelessness becomes a factor in their social identity, both in how they see themselves, and how other people see and react to them. The stigmatised identity influences how people construct and manage their behaviour on the basis of the meaning *they* have assigned to that identity; and it can change how others interpret his or her behaviour, irrespective of what the behaviour actually is.

In order to manage the impact of stigma, some people disengage with the spoiled identity linked to homelessness. Research has found that one way individuals try to avoid prejudicial responses is to hide their stigma and pass as 'part of the dominant group and thereby feign normalcy'[23]. The idea of 'passing' is central to the way some individuals try to reduce the inconsistency between how they want other people see them and their lived experience of being homeless. Passing creates specific patterns of interaction and daily routines (such as avoiding other homeless people and their locales) that reflect conscious decisions to resist homelessness.

Take for instance the example of women experiencing homelessness as a result of domestic violence. Most were acutely aware of the stigma of homelessness and what it 'said about you as a mother'. Most women in this study responded to the stigma by attempting to retain as many elements of normality in their daily lives as they could, and by distancing themselves from 'those other homeless people.' When they spoke about homelessness they perpetuated stereotypical images of the homeless as drunks, 'druggies' or in some way dysfunctional and, by definition, different from them.

The practice of passing implies that people have internalised the negative views of mainstream society, and are seeking acceptance by concealing their situation. However, a different response to managing stigma occurs when acceptance is sought from other homeless people. Recent research shows that many people who experience stigma commonly have a different view of stigma to what the mainstream might imagine; and, rather than distancing themselves, some people respond to stigma by connecting with others in similar circumstances.

This connecting response creates a different set of routines and social interactions. Individuals who 'embrace' homelessness in this way commonly become involved in a homeless subculture. Through interaction with other people in similar situations, a homeless subculture provides an alternative source of social validation and security, and can help suppress some of the anxiety typically associated with being homeless. For example, many young people inverted the stigma of homelessness so that they connected to and positively identified with other people in similar circumstances. The tragedy is that this response, while providing a needed sense of belonging and social validation, commonly locked them into the homeless population for significant periods of time. Through interaction with the homeless subculture, new routines emerge and through these routines 'homelessness starts to become normal'[24]. Over time, routines embed people, both behaviourally and cognitively, in the homeless subculture.

The important point to emphasise is that people actively respond to and manage the impact of stigma. These different responses generate different social practices for people on each pathway, and have unique consequences for their experience and duration of homelessness.

'Normality' is a heavily laden term and, while it is rarely used in sociological research*, it features strongly in research

---

* In his analysis of inmates in mental hospitals Goffman (1961) summarises his view of normalcy in the following way. 'It was then and still is my belief that any group of persons ... develop a life of their own that becomes meaningful, reasonable and normal once you get close to it.' In his work on stigma Goffman's (1963) view on 'normality' expresses the sentiment we are trying to capture with the term normal. Goffman states that the notion of the 'normal human being' may have its source in the medical approach to humanity or the tendency of large-scale bureaucratic organisations, such as the nation-state, to treat all members in some respects as equals. Whatever its origins, it seems to provide the basic imagery which many laymen conceive of themselves.

in which the voices of homeless people are included[25, 26]. The idea of 'normality' featured strongly in the distancing strategies used by people to get out of homelessness. It is also important to recognise the link between 'normality' and people's reaction to the stigma of homelessness. While few Australian studies consider stigma from a structural perspective (or from any perspective for that matter), overseas studies that do, focus primarily on the negative effects of stigma. Yet this study shows that people respond to stigmatised statuses in different ways. In their study of stigma Miller and Kaiser[27] argue that many stigmatised people continue to function 'as well as other people despite the fact they are disadvantaged'. This was true among many individuals interviewed for this study. Rather than presume that stigmatised individuals respond in similar ways, it is important to get an insider's view of stigma in order to understand how different groups manipulate stigma to make sense of *their* world. Thinking about stigma in this way emphasises the active role people play in shaping their social reality and avoids treating the homeless as 'objects or victims of prejudice'[28].

Subculture

Along with stigma, the homeless subculture is an important concept for explaining the experience of homelessness. The homeless subculture is not a physical structure, but consists of rules, values, practices and shared experiences that influence the nature of homeless people's interactions with other homeless people, with people who are housed and, ultimately, their experience of homelessness. Unlike many other subcultures that are defined by shared belief systems, the homeless subculture is characterised more by a response to common, adverse circumstances.

Many studies of persistent homelessness have identified a process of acculturation that occurs as people start to engage with the homeless subculture[29]. One explanation of prolonged or chronic homelessness is the increasing acceptance of the norms and values of the homeless population. According to this approach the primary factor that prolongs homelessness is identification with and, ultimately, acceptance of homelessness as a way of life. People who engage with the homeless subculture adapt behaviourally and cognitively over time and eventually homelessness becomes routinised or normal. This makes it increasingly difficult to get out and stay out of homelessness.

Starting in the US, this approach has a long lineage. In 1936 Edwin Sutherland and Harvey Locke wrote their influential account, *Twenty Thousand Homeless Men: A Study of Unemployed Men in the Chicago Shelters*. They argued that most individuals who used emergency accommodation initially did so with the expectation of it being a temporary arrangement. They theorised that a process of 'shelterization' took place over time – the longer men stayed in the shelter, the more dispirited they became by the impact of repeated rejection by employers, which in turn lowered their resistance to the lassitude and resignation that characterised the subculture of the shelter.

In the late 1950s Samuel Wallace (1965) applied the theory of subcultural identification to the problem of skid row in Minneapolis. He recognised that poverty, on its own, was an insufficient explanation for why some impoverished men live on skid row while others don't; and he was also particularly critical of explanations that focused on alcoholism, unemployment and criminal activity, pointing out that many of these problems arose as a consequence of skid row life. Wallace theorised that increasing participation and identification with the skid row way of life was a product of two distinct social processes: rejection and attraction. He established a three-stage model that outlined the process leading to entrenchment in skid row. The first was exposure to skid row, which was followed by participation in the skid row community. The final stage involved increasing conformity to skid row values and the rejection of societal values[30]. In Australia, Chamberlain and Mackenzie[31] have also used the idea of a homeless subculture, although they focus entirely on homeless young people.

The effective use of the concept requires a definition that can be confidently measured, and we used the framework below to do this.

Defining the homeless subculture

While there is no definitive account of the homeless subculture, five themes or indicators consistently emerge from studies interested in the homeless subculture. They are: cognitive orientation, present orientation, resource sharing, adaptive responses and the use of the homelessness service system. Table A2 lists the five indicators and the characteristics used to measure them.

There are seven measures of cognitive orientation. The first three establish the extent to which people's social networks include other homeless people. The final four establish the extent to which people identify with others in similar circumstances.

Table A2 A framework for assessing the homeless subculture

Indicator	Measure
Cognitive orientation	Know homeless people
	Homeless friends
	Frequency of contact with other homeless people
	Describe yourself as homeless
	Identify with other homeless people
	Anything in common with the homeless
	Believes there is a negative stigma attached to homelessness
Present orientation	Exit planning (housing)
	Problem resolution
Resource sharing	Material (money, cigarettes)
	Survival information (rules, hierarchies)
Adaptive responses	Criminal activity (incarceration)
	Substance use
Use of homelessness services	Number of times in crisis or transitional accommodation

The second indicator, present orientation, reflects reports from homeless agencies that the homeless subculture is focused on 'day-to-day existence'[32]. This generally means that there is 'little or no planning' and there is always a 'last minute immediacy or urgency about their needs'. In order to gauge the degree of present orientation, the first interview asked people about the type of housing they were planning to exit to, and their thoughts on whether their 'problems' would be resolved by the time they exited transitional accommodation.

The third indicator of engagement with the homeless subculture is sharing resources with other people in similar

---

* Snow and Anderson (1993:170) characterise this day-to-day, moment-by-moment existence as a 'present orientation'.

circumstances. Resources can be material ones such as cigarettes, drinks, money or clothes but can also include sharing information and knowledge, which is particularly important in terms of cultural reproduction.

The fourth indicator captures adaptive responses. While involvement with the homeless subculture can provide psychological and material support, some adaptive behaviours, such as substance use, can reduce the capacity and the opportunities to secure and maintain permanent accommodation. These adaptive responses highlight the internal contradiction that while acculturation to homelessness can help people to cope with homelessness, certain adaptations can be 'doubly disadvantageous with respect to making a permanent exit from homelessness'[33]. Furthermore, financing problematic substance use can lead to other behavioural adaptations such as crime.

The final indicator of engagement with the homeless subculture is patterns of service usage in the homelessness service system. As part of a broader welfare system the extent, nature and style of services available to the homeless has always been an important factor in the day-to-day lives of homeless people[34, 35]. Apart from its formal role in assisting people out of homelessness it is also important to consider the way in which the homelessness service system might reproduce the homeless subculture and inadvertently perpetuate the conditions that homeless people are trying to escape.

How homeless people relate to the homeless subculture has an important bearing on what happens to them when they are homeless and also has important consequences in terms of changes to people's cognitive and behavioural orientation. Typically, research has shown that people adapt more to homelessness the longer they stay in the population. In clear contrast, however, this book shows that people on the mental health pathway do not identify with homelessness and nonetheless experience the longest duration of all the groups. This research provides a more nuanced analysis by focusing attention on the way people's pre-homeless experiences and their pathway into homelessness mediate both the experience and duration of homelessness.

Although it is clear that different responses to homelessness are linked to the extent an individual's social network includes other homeless people, the composition of these networks is also influenced by the pathway individuals travelled into homelessness. In future, researchers interested in examining variations in the dynamic patterning of homelessness may consider what factors influence changes to the 'network structures' of homeless people and how changes in those networks influence, or are influenced by, movement in and out of the homeless population.

Variations in homelessness can be explained by recognising that people either 'reject' or 'embrace' homelessness depending on how they view and respond to the stigma attached to homelessness, and how they respond to the homeless subculture. How people respond to these two structures locates them in different social contexts where different routines emerge. These routines have consequences for people when they are homeless, as well as having different consequences in terms of getting out and staying out of the homeless population.

ROUTINES

Daily life is made up of a great number of little routines that provide connection and meaning, as well as the stability essential for psychological and emotional wellbeing – getting up at a certain time each day, eating the breakfast that you like and going to the job that provides you with financial security and social interaction. Routines can breed boredom, but they also establish social identities and their associated opportunities. Routines link us to a network of social relations and consequently mediate between an individual and society.

On the one hand, individuals actively engage with and shape the social system in which they exist through their daily routines. On the other hand, daily activities are both constrained and enabled by structural factors. Routines are, more or less, the rhythm or the flow of daily life; they are the familiar, reassuring processes that position us in a range of social contexts such as the workplace, school, family, friends and neighbourhoods.

Routines are also a vital psychological mechanism whereby a sense of trust or ontological security is nurtured and sustained. Of course, routines frequently change, but the key issue is the level of individual control and consent. Most changes, such as when children go to school for the first time, are predictable. Going to school for the first time involves disruption for both parent and child but, over time, parents and children re-establish new routines and interactions associated with the new locale. In contrast, during what Anthony Giddens called a 'critical situation', daily life is so seriously disrupted that trust in the predictability, continuity and permanence of our social context can be broken[36]. Whether the disruption occurs because of changes in external conditions or because of the actions of individuals, what commonly follows is a period of 'heightened anxiety'[37] as people try to adjust to their new social circumstances and the new social identity attached to those circumstances.

Becoming homeless is a 'critical situation' for many households, but this is not always the case. For instance, for some young people escaping abusive family relationships, becoming homeless is not a critical situation in that sense because their home was not a place of security to start with. Nevertheless, whether the experience of becoming homeless constitutes a critical disruption or not, pre-existing routines are broken during the process and people have to rebuild their routines in an entirely new social context.

Whichever pathway people travel on, becoming homeless involves a disruption to existing routines, and new routines begin to form once people are homeless. In the process of becoming homeless, people necessarily deal with the disruption to their existing routines*.

The five pathways can be distinguished by the impact on routines. For people on some pathways, homelessness is a major disruption to their routines. Conversely, homelessness itself imposes or enables its own set of routines as people establish themselves and try to either overcome or adapt to their situation. Understanding the persistence of homelessness is assisted by

* The idea of routinisation is taken from Giddens' (1984) theory of structuration.

the idea of routinisation, or the process by which something is made to be everyday, normal or routine[*] [38]. Long durations of homelessness can result when homelessness becomes routinised. The five pathways identified from biographical information help to explain how homelessness becomes routinised for some households and not for others.

---

[*] The concepts of routine and routinisation stem from the work of Max Weber. In German the original terms are *Alltag*, which stands for the everyday, and *Veralltaglichung*, which literally means the process by which something is made to be everyday.

NOTES

Introduction

1   Chamberlain, C and D Mackenzie, 2003, 'Counting the Homeless 2001', Australian Bureau of Statistics, Canberra.

2   Hanover Welfare Services, 2006, 'Public Perceptions', Hanover Welfare Services, Melbourne.

3   Snow, D and L Anderson, 1993, *Down on their Luck: A study of homeless street people*, University of California Press, Berkeley.

4   Shlay, A and P Rossi, 1992, 'Social Science Research and Contemporary Studies of Homelessness', *Annual Review of Sociology*, vol 18, pp 129–160.

5   Neil, C and R Fopp, 1993, *Homelessness in Australia: Causes and Consequences*, CSIRO, Victorian Ministerial Advisory Committee on Homelessness and Housing.

6   Rossi, P, 1989, *Down and Out in America: The Origins of Homelessness*, 1989, Chicago University Press, Chicago.

7   Baldwin, D, 1998, 'The Substance Adaptation of Homeless Mentally Ill Women', *Human Organization*, vol 57(2), pp 190–199.

8   Momeni, J (ed.), 1990, *Homelessness in the United States – Data and Issues*, Praeger, New York.

9   Phelan, J and B Link, 1999, 'Who are "the Homeless"? Reconsidering the Stability and Composition of the Homeless Population', *American Journal of Public Health*, vol 89(9).

10 Chung, D, R Kennedy, B O'Brien and S Wendt, 2001, 'The Impact of Domestic and Family Violence on Women and Homelessness: Findings from a National Research Project', in *Out of the Fire: Domestic Violence and Homelessness*, Council to Homeless Persons, Melbourne.

11 Rossiter, B, S Mallett, P Myers and D Rosenthal, 2003, 'Living Well? Homeless young people in Melbourne', Australian Research Centre in Sex, Health and Society, Melbourne.

12 Argeriou, M, M McCarty and K Mulvey, 1995, 'Dimensions of Homelessness', *Public Health Reports*, vol 110, pp 734–741.

13 Piliavin, I, H Westerfelt and E Elliott, 1989, 'Estimating Mental Illness among the Homeless: The Effects of Choice-Based Sampling', *Social Problems*, vol 36(5).

14 Snow, D, S Baker and L Anderson, 1989, 'Criminality and Homeless Men: An Empirical Assessment', *Social Problems*, vol 36(5), pp 532–549.

15 Teeson, M, T Hodder and N Buhrich, 2000, 'Substance abuse disorders among homeless people in inner Sydney', *Social Psychiatry*, vol 35, pp 451–456.

16 Bassuk, E, *et al.* 1997, 'Homelessness in Female-Headed Families: Childhood and Adult Risk and Protective Factors', *American Journal of Public Health*, vol 87(2).

17 Horn, M, 1999, *Drugs and Homelessness: The Prevalence of Alcohol and Drug Dependence among People experiencing Homelessness*, Hanover Welfare Services, Melbourne.

18 Baron, S, 1999, 'Street youth and substance abuse: The role of background, street lifestyle, and economic factors', *Youth and Society*, vol 31(1), pp 3–32.

19 Neale, J, 2001, 'Homelessness amongst drug users: A double jeopardy explored', *The International Journal of Drug Policy*, vol 12, pp 353–369.

20 Dalton, T and J Rowe, 2002, 'A Wasting Resource: Public Housing and Drug Use in Inner City Melbourne', Housing, Crime and Stronger Communities Conference, Melbourne.

21 Bassuk, E, L Rubin and A Lauriat, 1984, 'Is Homelessness a Mental Health Problem?' *American Journal of Psychiatry*, vol 141, pp 1546–1549.

22 Burt, M and B Cohen, 1989, 'Differences among Homeless Single Women, Women with Children, and Single Men', *Social Problems*, vol 36(5), pp 508–523.

23 Bassuk, *et al.* 1997.

24 Roman N and P Wolfe, 1997, 'The Relationship between Foster Care and Homelessness', *Public Welfare*, vol 55(1).

25 Zlotnick, C, M Robertson and M Lahiff, 1999, 'Getting off the Streets: Economic Resources and Residential Exits from Homelessness', *Journal of Community Psychology*, vol 27(2), pp 209–224.

26 Zlotnick, C, D Kronstadt and L Klee, 1998, 'Foster Care Children and Family Homelessness', *American Journal of Public Health*, vol 88 (9).

27 Johnson, G, 2006, 'On the Move: A Longitudinal Study of Pathways In and Out of Homelessness', School of Global Studies, Social Science and Planning, RMIT University, Melbourne.

28 Culhane, D, 2005, 'Translating Research into Homelessness Policy and Practice: One Perspective from the United States', *Parity*, vol 18(10), p 19.

29 Johnson, G, 2006.

30 Clapham, D, 2003, 'Pathways Approaches to Homeless Research', *Journal of Community and Applied Social Psychology*, vol 13, pp 119–127.

31 Clapham, D, 2002, 'Housing Pathways: A Post Modern Analytical Framework', *Housing, theory and society*, vol 19, pp 57–68.

Chapter 1: Pathways into homelessness

1 National Youth Coalition for Housing, 1999, 'Accommodating Homeless Young People with Mental Health Issues', National Research Project, Department of Family and Community Services, Canberra.

2 Laing, L, 2000b, 'Progress, trends and challenges in Australian responses to domestic violence', Issues Paper 1, Australian Domestic and Family Violence Clearing House, NSW.

3 *ibid.*

4 Gregory, R, 2001, 'Revisiting Domestic Violence and Homelessness', in *Out of the Fire: Domestic Violence and Homelessness*, Council to Homeless Persons, Melbourne.

5 Adkins, B, K Barnett, K Jerome, M Heffernan and J Minnery, 2003, *Women, Housing and Transitions out of Homelessness: A Report for The Commonwealth Office of the Status of Women*, AHURI, Queensland.

6   Dupuis, A and D Thorns, 1998, 'Home, home ownership and the search for ontological security', *The Sociological Review*, vol 46(1), pp 24–47.

7   Watson, S, 2001, 'Homelessness Revisited: New Reflections on Old Paradigms', *Urban Policy and Research*, vol 82(2), pp 159–170.

8   Cibich, G, 2001, 'The Port Lincoln Domestic Violence Rapid Response', in *Out of the Fire: Domestic Violence and Homelessness*, Council to Homeless Persons, Melbourne.

9   Adkins, B, *et al.* 2003.

10 Murray, S, 2002, *More than a Refuge: Changing Responses to Domestic Violence*, University of Western Australia Press, Perth.

11 Laing, L, 2000b.

12 Lawrence, C, 2001, 'Challenging Orthodoxies: The Next Step', in *Out of the Fire: Domestic Violence and Homelessness*, Council to Homeless Persons, Melbourne.

13 Metraux, S and D Culhane, 1999, 'Family Dynamics, Housing and Recurring Homelessness Among Women in New York City Homeless Shelters', *Journal of Family Issues*, vol 20(3), pp 371–396.

14 Laing, L, 2000a, *Children, young people and domestic violence*, Issues Paper 2, Australian Domestic Violence Clearing House, NSW.

15 Edwards, S, 2001, 'Domestic Violence and Homelessness: What are the Legal Parameters?', in *Out of the Fire: Domestic Violence and Homelessness*, Council to Homeless Persons, Melbourne.

16 Neil, C and R Fopp, 1993, *Homelessness in Australia: Causes and Consequences*, CSIRO, Victorian Ministerial Advisory Committee on Homelessness and Housing.

17 Saunders, P, Y Naidoo and M Griffiths, 2007, 'Towards New Indicators of Disadvantage: Deprivation and Social Exclusion in Australia', Social Policy Research Centre, University of New South Wales.

18 Human Rights and Equal Opportunity Commission, 1989, *Our Homeless Children*, Australian Government Publishing Service, Canberra.

19 Neil, C and R Fopp, 1993.

20 Henderson, R, 1975, *Commission of Inquiry into Poverty, First Main Report*, Australian Government Publishing Service, Canberra.

21 Yates, J and G Wood, 2005, 'Affordable Rental Housing: Lost, Stolen and Strayed', *The Economic Record*, vol 81(255) pp 82–95.

22 Rossi, P, 1989, *Down and Out in America: The Origins of Homelessness*, Chicago University Press, Chicago.

23 Marks, R, 1989, 'Prohibition or Regulation: An Economist's View of Australian Heroin Policy', in *Fifth Annual Conference of the Australian and New Zealand Society of Criminology*, University of Sydney, New South Wales.

24 Rowe, J, 2002b, 'Survival Strategies of the Homeless and Drug Dependent', in *Housing, Crime and Stronger Communities Conference*, Australian Institute of Criminology and Australian Housing and Urban Research Institute, Melbourne.

25 Mallet, S, J Edwards, D Keys, P Myers and D Rosenthal, 2003, 'Disrupting Stereotypes: Young people, drug use and homelessness', Key Centre for Women's Health in Society, The University of Melbourne, Melbourne.

26 Victorian Government, 1992, 'Making a Difference: A Progress Report on Youth Homelessness', Victorian Government, Melbourne.

27 Sykes, H, 1993, *Youth Homelessness: Courage and Hope*, Melbourne University Press, Melbourne.

28 House of Representatives, 1995, *A Report on Aspects of Youth Homelessness*, Australian Government Publishing Service, Canberra.

29 Hier, S, P Korboot and R Schweitzer, 1990, 'Social adjustment and symptomology in two types of homeless adolescents: Runaways and throwaways', *Adolescence*, vol 25(100), pp 761–771.

30 Meadowcroft, G and D Charman, 2000, 'A psychological study of young women', *The Australian Educational and Development Psychologist*, vol 17(2), pp 70–81.

31 National Committee for the Evaluation of the Youth Services Support Scheme, 1983, 'One step forward: Youth Homelessness and Emergency Accommodation Services', Australian Government Publishing Services, Canberra.

32 O'Connor, I, 1989, *Our Homeless Children: Their Experiences*, 1989, Human Rights and Equal Opportunity Commission, Sydney.

33 *ibid.*

34 Crane, P and J Brannock, 1996, 'Homelessness among Young People in Australia: Early Intervention and Prevention – A Report to the National Youth Affairs Research Scheme', National Clearing House for Youth Studies, Hobart.

35 Hutson, S and M Liddiard, 1994, *Youth Homelessness, The Construction of a Social Issue*, MacMillan, London.

36 Randal, G, 1980, *No way Home: Homeless Young people in Central London*, Centrepoint Soho, London.

37 Mackenzie, D and C Chamberlain, 2003, *Homeless Careers: Pathways in and out of homelessness*, Swinburne and RMIT Universities, Melbourne.

38 Sykes, H, 1993.

39 Hutson, S and M Liddiard, 1994.

40 Hirst, C, 1989, *Forced Exit: A Profile of the Young and Homeless in Inner Urban Melbourne*, The Salvation Army, Melbourne.

41 Avramov, D, 1999, 'The State-of-the-art Research of Homelessness and Provision of Services in Europe', in *Coping with Homelessness: Issues to be Tackled and Best Practices in Europe*, Ashgate, Aldershot.

Chapter 2: On the 'go' – homeless experiences of substance users

1 Moore, D, 2004, 'Beyond "subculture" on the ethnography of illicit drug use', *Contemporary Drug Problems*, vol 31(2), pp 181–212.

2 Milburn, N, 1990, 'Drug Abuse among homeless people', in *Homelessness in the United States: Data and Issues*, Praeger, New York.

3 Bartholomew, T, 1999, *A Long Way from Home: Family Homelessness in the Current Welfare Context*, The Salvation Army, St Kilda.

4 Hoch, C and R Slayton, 1989, *New Homelessness and Old: Community and the Skid Row Hotel*, Temple University Press, Philadelphia.

5   Jope, S, 2000, *On the threshold: The future of private rooming houses in the City of Yarra*, Brotherhood of St Laurence, Melbourne.

6   Harvey, C, H Evert , H Herrman, T Pinzone and O Gurele, 2002, 'Disability, homelessness and social relationships among people living with psychosis in Australia', *National Survey of Mental Health and Wellbeing Bulletin*, Commonwealth Department of Health and Ageing, Canberra.

7   Snow, D and L Anderson, 1993, *Down on their Luck: A study of homeless street people*, University of California Press, Berkeley.

8   Rowe, J, 2002b, 'Survival Strategies of the Homeless and Drug Dependent', in *Housing, Crime and Stronger Communities Conference of the Australian and New Zealand Society of Criminology*, University of Sydney, New South Wales.

9   Rowe, J, 2002a, 'Heroin epidemic! Drugs and the moral panic in the western suburbs of Melbourne', *Just Policy*, vol 27, pp 38–45.

10 Giddens, A, 1979, *Central problems in social theory: Action, structure and contradiction in social analysis*, University of California Press, Berkeley.

11 Rossi, P, 1989, *Down and Out in America: The Origins of Homelessness*, Chicago University Press, Chicago.

12 Henderson, N, J Ross, S Darke, M Teesson and M Lynskey, 2002, 'Longitudinal studies of dependent heroin users in Australia: Feasibility and benefits', Monograph No. 49, National Drug and Alcohol Research Centre, University of New South Wales, Sydney.

13 O'Connor, G, L Wurmser, T Brown and J Smith, 1972, 'The Economics of Heroin Addiction: A New Interpretation of the Facts', in *It's So Good, Don't Even Try It Once: Heroin in Perspective*, Prentice-Hall Inc, Englewood Cliffs, New Jersey.

14 Bessant, J, H Coupland, T Dalton, L Maher, J Rowe and R Watts, 2002, 'Heroin users, housing and social participation: Attacking social exclusion through better housing', AHURI, Melbourne.

15 Baldry, E, D MacDonald, P Maplestone and M Peeters, 2002, 'Ex-Prisoners and Accommodation: What bearing do different forms of housing have on the social reintegration of ex-prisoners?', *Housing, Crime and Stronger Communities Conference*, Melbourne.

16 Metraux, S and D Culhane, 2004, 'Homeless Shelter Use and Reincarceration Following Prison Release', *Criminology and Public Policy*, vol 3(2), pp 139–60.

17 Saunders, P, 2004, *Australia's welfare habit and how to kick it*, Centre for Independent Studies, St Leonards, New South Wales.

18 Rowe, J, 2002b, 'Survival Strategies of the Homeless and Drug Dependent', in *Housing, Crime and Stronger Communities Conference*, Australian Institute of Criminology and Australian Housing and Urban Research Institute, Melbourne.

19 O'Dwyer, B, 1997, 'Pathways to Homelessness: A Comparison of Gender and Schizophrenia in Inner-Sydney', *Australian Geographical Studies*, vol 35(3), pp 294–307.

20 Thompson Goodall and Associates, 1999a, 'Understanding Demand for Crisis Accommodation: A Snapshot Analysis of Current Demand on Major Crisis Accommodation Services in Inner Urban Melbourne', Melbourne.

21 NSW Ombudsman, 2004, 'Assisting homeless people – the need to improve their access to accommodation and support services', Final report arising from an Inquiry

into access to, and exiting from, the Supported Accommodation Assistance Program, Sydney, New South Wales.

22 Link, B and J Phelan, 2001, 'Conceptualizing Stigma', *American Review of Sociology*, vol 27, pp 363–385.

Chapter 3: Homeless careers of the mentally ill

1   Bartholemew, T, 1999, *A Long Way from Home: Family Homelessness in the Current Welfare Context*, The Salvation Army, St Kilda.

2   Harvey, C, H Evert, H Herrman, T Pinzone and O Gurele, 2002, 'Disability, homelessness and social relationships among people living with psychosis in Australia', in *National Survey of Mental Health and Wellbeing Bulletin*, Commonwealth Department of Health and Ageing, Canberra.

3   Merton, R, 1968, *Social Theory and Social Structure*, The Free Press, New York.

4   Goffman, E, 1963, *Stigma: Notes on the Management of Spoiled Identity*, Penguin Books, Ringwood, Victoria.

5   Phelan, J, B Link, R Moore and A Stueve, 1997, 'The stigma of homelessness: The impact of the label "Homelessness" on attitudes towards poor persons', *Social Psychology Quarterly*, vol 60(4), pp 323–337.

6   Harvey, C *et al.* 2002.

7   Davidson, L and D Stayner, 1997, 'Loss, Loneliness and the Desire for Love: Perspectives on the Social Lives of People with Schizophrenia', *Psychiatric Rehabilitation Journal*, vol 20, pp 3–12.

8   Albert, M, T Becker, P McCrone and G Thornicroft, 1998, 'Social networks and mental health service utilisation: A literature review', *International Journal of Social Psychiatry*, vol 16(1), pp 1–22.

9   NSW Ombudsman, 2004, 'Assisting homeless people – the need to improve their access to accommodation and support services', Final report arising from an inquiry into access to, and exiting from, the Supported Accommodation Assistance Program, Sydney, New South Wales.

10 Koegel, P, 1992, 'Through a different lens: An anthropological perspective on the homeless mentally ill', *Culture, Medicine and Psychiatry* (Historical Archive), vol 16(1), pp 1–22.

11 Baldwin, D, 1998, 'The Subsistence Adaptation of Homeless Mentally Ill Women', *Human Organization*, vol 57(2), pp 190–199.

12 O'Dwyer, B, 1997, 'Pathways to Homelessness: A Comparison of Gender and Schizophrenia in Inner Sydney', *Australian Geographical Studies*, vol 35(3), pp 294–307.

13 Leal, D, M Galanter, H Dermatis and L Westreich, 1998, 'Correlates of Protracted Homelessness in a Sample of Dually Diagnosed Psychiatric Inpatients', *Journal of Substance Abuse Treatment*, vol 16(2), pp 143–147.

14 Hodder, T, M Teesson and N Buhrich, 1988, *Down and Out In Sydney: Prevalence of mental disorders, disability and health service use among homeless people in inner Sydney*, Sydney City Mission, Sydney.

Chapter 4: Experiences on the domestic violence and housing crisis pathways

1   Harter, L, C Berquist, S Titsworth, D Novak and T Brokaw, 2005, 'The Structuring of Invisibility Among the Hidden Homeless: The Politics of Space, Stigma, and Identity Construction, *Journal of Applied Communication Research*, vol 33(4), pp 305–327.

2   Appelbaum, R, 1990, 'Counting the Homeless', *Homelessness in the United States: Data and Issues*, Praeger, New York.

3   Watson, S, 2001, 'Homelessness Revisited: New Reflections on Old Paradigms', *Urban Policy and Research*, vol 18(2), pp 159–170.

4   Wright, B, A Caspi, T Moffitt and P Silvia, 1998, 'Factors Associated with Doubled-Up Housing: A Common Precursor to Homelessness', *Social Service Review*, vol 72(1), pp 92–111.

5   Wong, I, 1997, 'Patterns of Homelessness: A Review of Longitudinal Studies', in *Understanding Homelessness: New policy and Research Perspectives*, Fannie Mae Foundation, Washington DC.

6   Wong, I and I Piliavin, 1997, 'A Dynamic Analysis of Homeless-Domicile Transitions', *Social Problems*, vol 44(3), pp 408–423.

7   Chamberlain, C and G Johnson, 2002a, 'Homeless Adults: Understanding Early Intervention', *Just Policy*, vol 26.

8   Link, B, E Susser, A Stueve, J Phelan, R Moore and E Struening, 1994, 'Lifetime and Five-year Prevalence of Homelessness in the United States', *American Journal of Public Health*, vol 84(12).

9   Access Economics, 2004, The Costs of Domestic Violence to the Australian Economy: Part 2, Office of the Status of Women, Canberra.

10 Access Economics, 2004, The Costs of Domestic Violence to the Australian Economy: Part 1, Office of the Status of Women, Canberra.

11 McChesney, K, 1990, 'Family Homelessness: A Systemic Problem', *Journal of Social Issues*, vol 46(4), pp 191–205.

12 Bartholomew, T, 1999, *A Long Way from Home: Family Homelessness in the Current Welfare Context*, The Salvation Army, St Kilda.

13 Vissing, Y,1990, *Out of Sight, Out of Mind: Homeless Children and Families in Small-town America*, The University Press of Kentucky, Kentucky.

14 Twaite, J and D Lampert, 1997, 'Outcomes of mandated preventative services program for homeless and truant children: A follow-up study', *Social Work*, vol 41(1), pp 11–18.

15 McCaughey, J, 1992, 'Where now? A Study of Homeless Families in the 1990s', Australian Institute of Family Studies Policy Background Paper No. 8, Australian Institute of Family Studies, Melbourne.

16 McCaughey, J, 1991, 'Nomads in a settled population: Families and homelessness', Australian Institute of Family Studies, Melbourne.

17 McCaughey, J, 1987, *A Bit of a Struggle: Coping with Family Life in Australia*, McPhee Gribble/Penguin Books, Melbourne.

18 Wagner, D, 1997, 'Reinterpreting the "Undeserving Poor": From Pathology to Resistance', in *International Critical Perspectives on Homelessness*, Praeger, New York.

19 Katz, M, 1993, 'The Urban Underclass as a Metaphor of Social Transformation', in *The Underclass Debate: Views from History*, Princeton University Press, Princeton, New Jersey.

20 Tracy, E and R Stoecker, 1993, 'Homelessness: The Service Providers' Perspective on Victim Blaming', *Journal of Sociology and Social Welfare*, vol 20(3), pp 43–59.

21 Rossi, P, 1989, *Down and Out in America: The Origins of Homelessness*, 1989, Chicago University Press, Chicago.

22 Snow, D and L Anderson, 1993, *Down on their Luck: A study of homeless street people*, University of California Press, Berkeley.

23 Neil, C and R Fopp, 1993, *Homelessness in Australia: Causes and Consequences*, CSIRO, Victorian Ministerial Advisory Committee on Homelessness and Housing.

24 Saunders, P, 2002, *The Ends and Means of Welfare: Coping with Economic and Social Change in Australia*, Cambridge University Press, Cambridge.

25 Link, B and J Phelan, 2001, 'Conceptualizing Stigma', *American Review of Sociology*, vol 27, pp 363–385.

26 Goffman, E, 1963, *Stigma: Notes on the Management of Spoiled Identity*, Penguin Books, Ringwood, Victoria.

27 Link, B and J Phelan, 2001.

28 Kaufman, J and C Johnson, 2004, 'Stigmatised Individuals and the Process of Identity', *The Sociological Quarterly*, vol 45(4), pp 807–833.

29 Shih, M, 2004, 'Positive Stigma: Examining Resilience and Empowerment in Overcoming Stigma', *The Annals of the American Academy*, vol 591 (January), pp 175–185.

30 Goffman, E, 1963.

Chapter 5: Transition to adult homelessness

1 Hutson, S and M Liddiard, 1994, *Youth Homelessness: The Construction of a Social Issue*, MacMillan, London.

2 Auerswald, C and S Eyre, 2002, 'Youth Homelessness in San Francisco: A life cycle approach', *Social Science and Medicine*, vol 54, pp 1497–1512.

3 Chamberlain, C and D Mackenzie, 1998, *Youth Homelessness: Early Intervention and Prevention*, Australian Centre for Equity through Education, Sydney.

4 Crane, P, and J Brannock, 1996, Homelessness among Young People in Australia: Early Intervention and Prevention – A Report to the National Youth Affairs Research Scheme, National Clearing House for Youth Studies, Hobart.

5 Smith, J, 1995, *Being young and homeless*, The Salvation Army, Melbourne.

6 Auerswald, C and S Eyre, 2002.

7 O'Connor, I, 1989, *Our Homeless Children: Their Experiences*, Human Rights and Equal Opportunity Commission, Sydney.

8 Chamberlain, C and D Mackenzie, 1998.

9 MacKenzie, D and C Chamberlain, 1995, 'The National Census of Homeless School Students', *Youth Studies Australia*, vol 14(1), pp22–28.

10 Craig, TKJ and S Hodson, 1998, 'Homeless youth in London: childhood antecedents and psychiatric disorder', *Psychological Medicine*, vol 28, pp1379–1388.

11 Smith, J, 1995, *Being young and homeless*, The Salvation Army, Melbourne.

12 *ibid.*

13 Crane, P, and J Brannock, 1996.

14 Chamberlain, C and D Mackenzie, 1998.

15 Thompson Goodall and Associates, Pty Ltd, 1999b, *Early Intervention in SAAP: A report prepared for the Department of Family and Community Services*, DFACS, Canberra.

16 Dwyer, P and J Wyn, 2001, *Youth, Education and Risk: Facing the Future*, Routledge/Falmer, London and New York.

17 Crago, H, 1991, 'Homeless Youth: How the Solution Becomes Part of the Problem', *Quadrant*, vol 35(9), pp 26–32.

18 Chamberlain, C and D Mackenzie, 1998.

19 Mallet, S, J Edwards, D Keys, P Myers and D Rosenthal, 2003, 'Disrupting Stereotypes: Young people, drug use and homelessness', Key Centre for Women's Health in Society, The University of Melbourne, Melbourne.

20 Hirst, C, 1989, *Forced Exit: A Profile of the Young and Homeless in Inner Urban Melbourne*, The Salvation Army, Melbourne.

21 Smith, J, 1995.

22 Mallet, S, *et al.* 2003.

23 Smith, J, 1995.

24 Burke, T, 1994, *Homelessness in Australia: Causal Factors*, Australian Government Publishing Service, Canberra.

25 Pinkey, S and S Ewing, 2006, 'The Costs and Pathways of Homelessness: Developing policy-relevant economic analyses for the Australian homelessness service system', Department of Families, Community Services and Indigenous Affairs, Canberra.

26 Hirst, C, 1989, *Forced Exit: A Profile of the Young and Homeless in Inner Urban Melbourne*, The Salvation Army, Melbourne.

27 *ibid.*

28 Burdekin, B, 1989, *Human rights and mental illness. Report of the National Inquiry into human rights of people with mental illness*, Human Rights and Equal Opportunity Commission, Australia.

29 Hirst, C, 1989.

30 Goffman, E, 1963, *Stigma: Notes on the Management of Spoiled Identity*, Penguin Books, Ringwood, Victoria.

31 Anderson, E, 1990, *Streetwise: Race, Class, and Change in an Urban Community*, Chicago University Press, Chicago.

32 Mallet, S, *et al.* 2003.

33 Baron, S, 1999, 'Street youth and substance abuse: The role of background, street lifestyle, and economic factors', *Youth and Society*, vol 31(1), pp 3–32.

34 Auerswald, C and S Eyre, 2002.

35 Carlson, J, E Sugano, S Millstein and C Auerswald, 2006, 'Service utilization and the life cycle of youth homelessness', *Journal of Adolescent Health*, vol 38, pp 624–627.

36 Baron, S, 1999.

37 Auerswald, C and S Eyre, 2002.

38 Mallet, S, *et al.* 2003.

39 Neil, C and R Fopp, 1993, *Homelessness in Australia: Causes and Consequences*, CSIRO, Victorian Ministerial Advisory Committee on Homelessness and Housing, Victoria.

40 Baron, S, 1999.

41 Hanover Welfare Services, 2006, *Public Perceptions*, Hanover Welfare Services, Melbourne.

42 Wolch, J, M Dear and A Akita, 1998, 'Explaining Homelessness', *Journal of the American Planning Association*, vol 54(4), pp 443–454.

43 Koegal, P, E Melamid and A Burnam, 1995, 'Childhood Risk Factors for Homelessness among Homeless Adults', *American Journal of Adolescent Health*, vol 85(12), pp 1624–1649.

44 Herman, D, E Susser, E Struening and B Link, 1997, 'Adverse Childhood Experiences: Are They Risk Factors for Adult Homelessness?', *American Journal of Public Health*, vol 87(2), pp 249–255.

45 Goffman, E, 1963.

46 Grigsby, C, D Baumann, S Gregorich and C Roberts-Grey, 1990, 'Disaffiliation to Entrenchment: A Model for Understanding Homelessness', *Journal of Social Issues*, vol 46(4), pp 141–156.

47 Auerswald, C and S Eyre, 2002.

48 Hier, S, P Korboot and R Schweitzer, 1990, 'Social adjustment and symptomology in two types of homeless adolescents: Runaways and throwaways', *Adolescence*, vol 25(100), pp 761–771.

49 Fine, G, 1992, 'Agency, Structure and Comparative Contexts: Towards a Synthetic Interactionism', *Symbolic Interaction*, vol 15(1), pp 87–107.

Chapter 6: Getting out and staying out

1 Wong, I, 1997, 'Patterns of Homelessness: A Review of Longitudinal Studies', in *Understanding Homelessness: New policy and Research Perspectives*, Fannie Mae Foundation, Washington DC.

2 Horn, M, 2002, 'Increasing Homelessness: Evidence of housing market failure in Australia', *Just Policy*, vol 25, pp 26–31.

3 Wallace, R and E Bassuk, 1991, 'Housing famine and homelessness: how the low income housing crisis affects families with inadequate supports', *Environment and Planning*, vol 23, pp 485–498.

4 Edgar B and J Doherty, 2001, 'Supported Housing and Homelessness in the European Union', *European Journal of Housing Policy*, vol 1(1), pp 59–78.

5 Sosin, M, I Piliavan and H Westerfelt, 1990, 'Toward a Longitudinal Analysis of Homelessness', *Journal of Social Issues*, vol 46(4), pp 157–174.

6   Wong, I, 1997.

7   Piliavin, I, B Wright, R Mare and A Westerfelt, 1996, 'Exits from and returns to Homelessness', *Social Service Review*, vol 70(1), pp 33–57.

8   Dworsky, AL and I Piliavin, 2000, 'Homeless Spells, Exits and Returns: Substantive and Methodological Elaborations on Recent Studies', *Social Service Review*, vol 74(2), pp 193–213.

9   Wong, I, D Culhane and R Kuhn, 1997, 'Predictors of Exit and Reentry among Homeless Family Shelter Users in New York City', *Social Service Review*, vol 74(3), pp 441–462.

10 Caton, C (ed.), 1990, *Homeless in America*, Oxford University Press, New York.

11 Craig, T, S Hodson, S Woodward and S Richardson, 1996, *Off to a bad start: a longitudinal study of homeless young people in London*, The Mental Health Foundation, London.

12 Horn, M and M Cooke, 2001, 'Hanover Family Outcomes Study: Profile of participating families and their experiences of homelessness', Hanover Welfare Services, Melbourne.

13 Burke, T and K Hulse, 2002, Allocating Social Housing, Swinburne-Monash AHURI Research Centre, Melbourne.

14 Salins, P, 2006, *The Concise Encyclopedia of Economics*, D Henderson (ed.), econlib.org/library/Enc/Housing.html

15 Wright-Howie, D, 2004, 'Public Housing in Australia is in Decline: The Facts Speak for Themselves', *Parity*, vol 17(10).

16 *ibid.*

17 Fischer, R, 2000, 'Towards Self-Sufficiency: Evaluating a Transitional Housing Program for Homeless Families', *Policy Studies Journal*, vol 28(2), pp 402–420.

18 Busch-Geertsema, V, 2005, 'Does Re-Housing lead to re-integration? Follow-up studies of re-housed homeless people', *Innovation: The European Journal of Social Science Research*, vol 18(2), pp 205–226.

19 La Gory, M, F Ritchey and K Fitzpatrick, 1991, 'Homelessness and Affiliation', *The Sociological Quarterly*, vol 32(2), pp 201–218.

20 Snow, D and L Anderson, 1993, *Down on their Luck: A study of homeless street people*, University of California Press, Berkeley.

21 Fitzpatrick, S, 2000, *Young Homeless People*, MacMillan, Basingstoke.

22 Edgar, B and J Doherty, 2001.

23 McNaughton, C, 2005, Crossing the Continuum: 'Understanding routes out of Homelessness and examining "what works"', Simon Community, Glasgow.

24 Anne Rosengard Associates, 2002, 'Routes out of Homelessness', Scottish Executive Central Research Unit, Edinburgh.

25 Morrissey, J and D Dennis, 1990, 'Homelessness and mental illness: Toward the next generation of research studies', National Institute of Mental Health, Rockville MD.

26 Fitzpatrick, S, 2000.

27 Susser, E, E Valencia, S Conover, A Felix, WY Tsai and RJ Wyatt, 1997, 'Preventing Recurrent Homelessness among Mentally Ill Men: A "Critical Time" Intervention after Discharge from a Shelter', *American Journal of Public Health*, vol 87(2), pp 256–262.

28 Fischer, R, 2000.

29 Victorian Homelessness Strategy, 2002, Action Plan and Strategic Framework: Directions for Change – A collaborative approach to improving our response to homelessness, Department of Human Services, Melbourne.

30 Department of Human Services, Victoria, 2002, Victorian Homelessness Strategy: Action Plan and Strategic Framework. Directions for Change: A collaborative approach to improving our response to homelessness, Melbourne.

31 Neale, J, 2001, 'Homelessness amongst drug users: A double jeopardy explored', *The International Journal of Drug Policy*, vol 12, pp 353–369.

32 Rice, E, N Milburn, MJ Rotheram-Borus, S Mallett and D Rosenthal, 2005, 'The Effects of Peer Group Network Properties on Drug Use Among Homeless Youth', *American Behavioural Scientist*, vol 48(8), pp 613–638.

33 Chamberlain, C and D Mackenzie, 1998, *Youth Homelessness: Early Intervention and Prevention*, Australian Centre for Equity through Education, Sydney.

34 Dworsky, AL and I Piliavin, 2000.

35 Horn, M and M Cooke, 2001, Hanover Family Outcomes Study: Profile of participating families and their experiences of homelessness, Hanover Welfare Services, Melbourne.

36 Susser, E, *et al.* 1997.

37 May, J, 2000, 'Housing Histories and Homeless Careers: A Biographical Approach', *Housing Studies*, vol 15(4), pp 613–638.

38 Piliavin, I, B Wright, R Mare and A Westerfelt, 1994, 'The Dynamics of Homelessness', Discussion Paper No. 1035-94, Institute for Research on Poverty, The University of Wisconsin-Madison.

39 Robinson, C, 2003, 'Understanding iterative homelessness: The case of people with mental disorders', Australian Housing and Urban Research Institute, Melbourne.

40 Westerfelt, H, 1990, 'The ins and outs of homelessness: Exit patterns and predictions', in *Graduate School – Social Welfare*, University of Wisconsin, Ann Arbor.

41 Caton, C (ed.), 1990.

42 May, J, 2000.

43 O'Flaherty, B, 1996, *Making Room: The economics of homelessness*, Harvard University Press, Cambridge, Massachusetts.

44 Snow, D and L Anderson, 1993.

45 *ibid.*

46 Rice, E, *et al.* 2005.

47 Baker and Smith, 1939, in Goffman, E, 1963, *Stigma: Notes on the Management of Spoiled Identity*, Penguin Books, Ringwood, Victoria.

48 Snow, D and L Anderson, 1993.

49 Goffman, E, 1963, *Stigma: Notes on the Management of Spoiled Identity*, Penguin Books, Ringwood, Victoria.

50 Metraux, S and D Culhane, 1999, 'Family Dynamics, Housing and Recurring Homelessness Among Women in New York City Homeless Shelters', *Journal of Family Issues*, vol 20(3), pp 371–396.

51 McChesney, K, 1990, 'Family Homelessness: A Systemic Problem', *Journal of Social Issues*, vol 46(4), pp 191–205.

52 Baum, A and D Burnes, 1993, 'Facing the facts about homelessness', *Public Welfare*, vol 51(2).

53 Adkins, B, K Barrett, K Jerome, M Heffernan and J Minnery, 2003, Women, Housing and Transitions out of Homelessness: A Report for the Commonwealth Office of the Status of Women, AHURI, Queensland.

54 Piliavin, I, M Sosin, A Westerfelt and R Matsueda, 1993, 'The Duration òf Homeless Careers: An Exploratory Study', *Social Service Review*, vol 67(4), pp 576–598.

55 Cohen, C, M Ramirez, J Teresi, M Gallagher and J Sokolovsky, 1997, 'Predictors of Becoming Redomiciled Among Older Homeless Women', *The Gerontologist*, vol 37(1), pp 67–74.

Chapter 7: How we should respond

1 Chamberlain, C, G Johnson and J Theobold, 2007, *Homelessness in Melbourne: Confronting the Challenge*, RMIT University, Melbourne.

2 Yates, J and M Gabriel, 2006, Housing affordability in Australia, National Research Venture 3: Housing affordability for lower income Australians, Australian Housing and Urban Research Institute, Melbourne.

3 Caton, C (ed.), 1990, *Homeless in America*, Oxford University Press, New York.

4 Chamberlain, C and G Johnson, 2002b, 'The Development of Prevention and Early Intervention Services for Homeless Youth: Intervening Successfully', Positioning Paper, AHURI, Melbourne.

5 Billis, D, 1981, 'At risk of prevention, *Journal of Social Policy*, vol 10(3), pp 367–379.

6 RPR Consulting, 2002, Making a Difference: First Report of the Longitudinal Evaluation of Reconnect, Sydney, NSW.

7 Fitzpatrick, S, 2000, *Young Homeless People*, MacMillan, Basingstoke.

8 Mendes, P and B Moslehuddin, 2004, 'Graduating from the child welfare system: a comparison of the UK and Australian leaving care debates', *International Journal of Social Welfare*, vol 13, pp 332–339.

9 Coleman, A, 2001, Five star motels: Spaces, places and homelessness in Fortitude Valley, *The School of Social Work and Applied Human Sciences*, University of Queensland, Brisbane.

10 Snow, D and L Anderson, 1993, *Down on their Luck: A study of homeless street people*, University of California Press, Berkeley.

11 Padgett, D, 2007, 'There's no place like (a) home: Ontological security among persons with a serious mental illness in the United States', *Social Science and Medicine*, vol 64, pp 1925–1936.

12 Padgett, D, L Gulcur and S Tsemberis, 2006, 'Housing First Services for People Who are Homeless With Co-Occurring Serious Mental Illness and Substance Abuse', *Research on Social Work*, vol 16(1), pp 74–83.

13 Tsemberis, S, 1999, 'From Streets to Homes: An Innovative Approach to Supported Housing for Homeless Adults with Psychiatric Disabilities', *Journal of Community Psychology*, vol 27(2), pp 225–241.

14 Tsemberis, S, L Gulcur and M Nakae, 2004, 'Housing First, Consumer Choice, and Harm Reduction for Homeless Individuals With a Dual Diagnosis', *American Journal of Public Health*, vol 94(4), pp 651–656.

Appendices

1 Wong, I, 1997, 'Patterns of Homelessness: A Review of Longitudinal Studies', in *Understanding Homelessness: New Policy and Research Perspectives*, Fannie Mae Foundation, Washington DC.

2 Sosin, M, I Piliavin and H Westerfelt, 1990, 'Toward a Longitudinal Analysis of Homelessness', *Journal of Social Issues*, vol 46(4), pp 157–174.

3 Piliavin, I, M Sosin, A Westerfelt and R Matsueda, 1993, 'The Duration of Homeless Careers: An Exploratory Study', *Social Service Review*, vol 67(4), pp 576–598.

4 Neil, C and R Fopp, 1993, *Homelessness in Australia: Causes and Consequences*, CSIRO, Victorian Ministerial Advisory Committee on Homelessness and Housing.

5 Crane, P and J Brannock, 1996, *Homelessness among Young People in Australia: Early Intervention and Prevention – A Report to the National Youth Affairs Research Scheme*, National Clearing House for Youth Studies, Hobart.

6 Chamberlain, C and D Mackenzie, 1992, 'Understanding Contemporary Homelessness: Issues of Definition and Meaning', *Australian Journal of Social Issues*, vol 27(4), pp 274–297.

7 Chamberlain, C and G Johnson, 2001, 'The Debate about Homelessness', *Australian Journal of Social Issues*, vol 39(1), pp 35–50.

8 Cordray, D and G Pion, 1997, 'What's Behind the Numbers? Definitional Issues in Counting the Homeless', in *Understanding Homelessness: New Policy and Research Perspectives*, Fannie Mae Foundation, Washington DC.

9 Chamberlain, C and D Mackenzie, 1992.

10 Avramov, D, 1999, 'The State-of-the-art Research of Homelessness and Provision of Services in Europe', in *Coping with Homelessness: Issues to be Tackled and Best Practices in Europe*, Ashgate, Aldershot.

11 Chamberlain, C and G Johnson, 2002a, 'Homeless Adults: Understanding Early Intervention', *Just Policy*, vol 26.

12 Burt, M, 1999, 'US Homeless Research During the 1980s and Early 1990s: Approaches, Lessons and Methodological Options', in *Coping with Homelessness: Issues to be Tackled and Best Practices in Europe*, Ashgate, Aldershot.

13 Huth, M, 1997, 'America's New Homeless', in *Critical International Perspectives on Homelessness*, Praeger, Westport, Connecticut.

14 Marcuse, P, 1996, 'Is Australia Different? Globalization and the New Urban Poverty', Occasional Paper 3, Australian Housing and Research Institute, Melbourne.

15 Hallebone, E, 1997, 'Homelessness and Marginality in Australia: Young and Old People Excluded from Independence', in *Critical International Perspectives on Homelessness*, Praeger, Westport, Connecticut.

16 Pinkey, S and S Ewing, 2006, *The Costs and Pathways of Homelessness: Developing policy-relevant economic analyses for the Australian homelessness service system*, Department of Families, Community Services and Indigenous Affairs, Canberra.

17 *ibid.*

18 Baron, S, 1999, 'Street youth and substance abuse: The role of background, street lifestyle, and economic factors', in *Youth and Society*, vol 31(1), pp 3–32.

19 Neil, C and R Fopp, 1993.

20 Robinson, C, 2003, 'Understanding iterative homelessness: The case of people with mental disorders', Australian Housing and Urban Research Institute, Melbourne.

21 Roschelle, A and P Kaufman, 2004, 'Fitting In and Fighting Back: Stigma Management Strategies among Homeless Kids', *Symbolic Interaction*, vol 27(1), p 23.

22 Phelan, J, B Link, R Moore and A Stueve, 1997, 'The stigma of homelessness: The impact of the label "Homeless" on attitudes towards poor persons', *Social Psychology Quarterly*, vol 60(4), pp 323–337.

23 Kaufman, J and C Johnson, 2004, 'Stigmatised Individuals and the Process of Identity', *The Sociological Quarterly*, vol 45(4), pp 807–833.

24 Cullen, P and CA Marshall, 1999, *Voices of the Street*, John Garrett Publishing, Melbourne.

25 Tosi, A, 2005, 'Rehousing and Social Integration of Homeless People: A case study from Milan', *Innovation: The European Journal of Social Science Research*, vol 18(2), pp 183–203.

26 Kennedy, C and S Fitzpatrick, 2001, 'Begging, Rough Sleeping and Social Exclusion: Implications for Social Policy', *Urban Studies*, vol 38(11), pp 2001–1016.

27 Miller, C and C Kaiser, 2001, 'A Theoretical Perspective on Coping with Stigma', *Journal of Social Issues*, vol 57(1), pp 73–92.

28 Oyserman, D and J Swim, 2001, 'Stigma: An Insider's View', *Journal of Social Issues*, vol 57(1), pp 1–14.

29 Piliavin, I, B Wright, R Mare and A Westerfelt, 1994, 'The Dynamics of Homelessness', Discussion Paper No. 1035-94, Institute for Research on Poverty, The University of Wisconsin-Madison.

30 Wallace, S, 1965, *Skid row as a way of life*, Bedminster Press, Totowa, NJ.

31 Chamberlain, C and D Mackenzie, 1998, *Youth Homelessness: Early Intervention and Prevention*, Australian Centre for Equity through Education, Sydney.

32 Bedford Street Outreach Service, 1997, Guide to Outreach, Melbourne.

33 Neil, C and R Fopp, 1993.

34 Hirst, C, 1989, *Forced Exit: A Profile of the Young and Homeless in Inner Urban Melbourne*, The Salvation Army, Melbourne.

35 Smith, J, 1995, *Being young and homeless*, The Salvation Army, Melbourne.

36 Giddens, A, 1984, *The Constitution of society: Outline of the theory of structuration*, University of California Press, Berkeley.

37 *ibid.*

38 Berger, P and B Berger, 1976, *Sociology: A Biographical Approach*, Penguin Books Ltd, Harmondsworth, UK.

BIBLIOGRAPHY

Adkins, B, K Barnett, K Jerome, M Heffernan and J Minnery, 2003, 'Women, Housing and Transitions out of Homelessness', A Report for The Commonwealth Office of the Status of Women, AHURI, Queensland.

Access Economics, 2004, 'The Costs of Domestic Violence to the Australian Economy: Part 1', Office of the Status of Women, Canberra.

Access Economics, 2004, 'The Costs of Domestic Violence to the Australian Economy: Part 2', Office of the Status of Women, Canberra.

Albert, M, T Becker, P McCrone and G Thornicroft, 1998, 'Social networks and mental heath service utilisation: A literature review', *International Journal of Social Psychiatry*, vol 16(1), pp 1–22.

Anderson, E, 1990, *Streetwise: Race, Class, and Change in an Urban Community*, Chicago University Press, Chicago.

Anne Rosengard Associates, 2002, Routes out of Homelessness, Scottish Executive Central Research Unit, Edinburgh.

Appelbaum, R, 1990, 'Counting the Homeless', in *Homelessness in the United States: Data and Issues*, Praeger, New York.

Argeriou, M, M McCarty and K Mulvey, 1995, 'Dimensions of Homelessness', *Public Health Reports*, vol 110, pp 734–741.

Auerswald, C and S Eyre, 2002, 'Youth Homelessness in San Francisco: A life cycle approach', *Social Science and Medicine*, vol 54, pp 1497–1512.

Avramov, D, 1999, 'The State-of-the-art Research of Homelessness and Provision of Services in Europe', in *Coping with Homelessness: Issues to be Tackled and Best Practices in Europe*, Ashgate, Aldershot.

Baker and Smith, 1939, in Goffman, E, 1963, *Stigma: Notes on the Management of Spoiled Identity*, Penguin Books, Ringwood, Victoria.

Baldry, E, D MacDonald, P Maplestone and M Peeters, 2002, 'Ex-Prisoners and Accommodation: What bearing do different forms of housing have on the social reintegration of ex-prisoners', *Housing, Crime and Stronger Communities Conference*, Melbourne.

Baldwin, D, 1998, 'The Substance Adaptation of Homeless Mentally Ill Women', *Human Organization*, vol 57(2), pp 190–199.

Baron, S, 1999, 'Street youth and substance abuse: The role of background, street lifestyle, and economic factors', *Youth and Society*, vol 31(1), pp 3–32.

Bartholomew, T, 1999, *A Long Way from Home: Family Homelessness in the Current Welfare Context*, The Salvation Army, St Kilda.

Bassuk, E, L Rubin and A Lauriat, 1984, 'Is Homelessness a Mental Health Problem?' *American Journal of Psychiatry*, vol 141, pp 1546–1549.

Bassuk, E, *et al.* 1997, 'Homelessness in Female-Headed Families: Childhood and Adult Risk and Protective Factors', *American Journal of Public Health*, vol 87(2).

Baum, A and D Burnes, 1993, 'Facing the facts about homelessness', *Public Welfare*, vol 51(2).

Bedford Street Outreach Service, 1997, Guide to Outreach, Melbourne.

Berger, P and B Berger, 1976, *Sociology: A Biographical Approach*, Penguin Books Ltd, Harmondsworth, UK.

Bessant, J, H Coupland, T Dalton, L Maher, J Rowe and R Watts, 2002, 'Heroin users, housing and social participation: Attacking social exclusion through better housing', AHURI, Melbourne.

Billis, D, 1981, 'At risk of prevention, *Journal of Social Policy*, vol 10(3), pp 367–379.

Burdekin, B, 1989, *Human rights and mental illness. Report of the National Inquiry into human rights of people with mental illness*, Human Rights and Equal Opportunity Commission, Australia.

Burke, T, 1994, *Homelessness in Australia: Causal Factors*, Australian Government Publishing Service, Canberra.

Burke, T and K Hulse, 2002, Allocating Social Housing, Swinburne-Monash AHURI Research Centre, Melbourne.

Burt, M and B Cohen, 1989, 'Differences among Homeless Single Women, Women with Children, and Single Men, *Social Problems*, vol 36(5), pp 508–523.

Burt, M, 1999, 'US Homeless Research During the 1980s and Early 1990s: Approaches, Lessons and Methodological Options', in *Coping with Homelessness: Issues to be Tackled and Best Practices in Europe*, Ashgate, Aldershot.

Busch-Geertsema, V, 2005, 'Does Re-Housing lead to re-integration? Follow-up studies of re-housed homeless people', *Innovation: The European Journal of Social Science Research*, vol 18(2), pp 205–226.

Carlson, J, E Sugano, S Millstein and C Auerswald, 2006, 'Service utilization and the life cycle of youth homelessness', *Journal of Adolescent Health*, vol 38, pp 624–627.

Caton, C (ed.), 1990, *Homeless in America*, Oxford University Press, New York.

Chamberlain, C and D Mackenzie, 1992, 'Understanding Contemporary Homelessness: Issues of Definition and Meaning', *Australian Journal of Social Issues*, vol 27(4), pp 274–297.

Chamberlain, C and D Mackenzie, 1998, *Youth Homelessness: Early Intervention and Prevention*, Australian Centre for Equity through Education, Sydney.

Chamberlain, C and G Johnson, 2001, 'The Debate about Homelessness', *Australian Journal of Social Issues*, vol 39(1), pp 35–50.

Chamberlain, C and G Johnson, 2002a, 'Homeless Adults: Understanding Early Intervention', *Just Policy*, vol 26.

Chamberlain, C and G Johnson, 2002b, 'The Development of Prevention and Early Intervention Services for Homeless Youth: Intervening Successfully', Positioning Paper, AHURI, Melbourne.

Chamberlain, C and D Mackenzie, 2003, 'Counting the Homeless 2001', Australian Bureau of Statistics, Canberra.

Chamberlain, C, G Johnson and J Theobold, 2007, *Homelessness in Melbourne: Confronting the Challenge*, RMIT University, Melbourne.

Chung, D, R Kennedy, B O'Brien and S Wendt, 2001, 'The Impact of Domestic and Family Violence on Women and Homelessness: Findings from a National Research Project', in *Out of the Fire: Domestic Violence and Homelessness*, Council to Homeless Persons, Melbourne.

Cibich, G, 2001, 'The Port Lincoln Domestic Violence Rapid Response', in *Out of the Fire: Domestic Violence and Homelessness*, Council to Homeless Persons, Melbourne.

Clapham, D, 2002, 'Housing Pathways: A Post Modern Analytical Framework', *Housing, theory and society*, vol 19, pp 57–68.

Clapham, D, 2003, 'Pathways Approaches to Homeless Research', *Journal of Community and Applied Social Psychology*, vol 13, pp 119–127.

Coleman, A, 2001, 'Five star motels: Spaces, places and homelessness in Fortitude Valley', The School of Social Work and Applied Human Sciences, University of Queensland, Brisbane.

Crago, H, 1991, 'Homeless Youth: How the Solution Becomes Part of the Problem', *Quadrant*, vol 35(9), pp 26–32.

Craig, T, S Hodson, S Woodward and S Richardson, 1996, *Off to a bad start: a longitudinal study of homeless young people in London*, The Mental Health Foundation, London.

Craig, TKJ and S Hodson, 1998, 'Homeless youth in London: childhood antecedents and psychiatric disorder', *Psychological Medicine*, vol 28, pp1379–1388.

Crane, P and J Brannock, 1996, *Homelessness among Young People in Australia: Early Intervention and Prevention – A Report to the National Youth Affairs Research Scheme*, National Clearing House for Youth Studies, Hobart.

Culhane, D, 2005, 'Translating Research into Homelessness Policy and Practice: One Perspective from the United States', *Parity*, vol 18(10), p 19.

Cullen, P and CA Marshall, 1999, *Voices of the Street*, John Garrett Publishing, Melbourne.

Dalton, T and J Rowe, 2002, 'A Wasting Resource: Public Housing and Drug Use in Inner City Melbourne', Housing, Crime and Stronger Communities Conference, Melbourne.

Davidson, L and D Stayner, 1997, 'Loss, Loneliness and the Desire for Love: Perspectives on the Social Lives of People with Schizophrenia', *Psychiatric Rehabilitation Journal*, vol 20, pp 3–12.

Department of Human Services, Victoria, 2002, Victorian Homelessness Strategy: Action Plan and Strategic Framework. Directions for Change: A collaborative approach to improving our response to homelessness, Melbourne.

Dupuis, A and D Thorns, 1998, 'Home, home ownership and the search for ontological security', *The Sociological Review*, vol 46(1), pp 24–47.

Dworsky, AL and I Piliavin, 2000, 'Homeless Spells, Exits and Returns: Substantive and Methodological Elaborations on Recent Studies', *Social Service Review*, vol 74(2), pp 193–213.

Dwyer, P and J Wyn, 2001, *Youth, Education and Risk: Facing the Future*, Routledge/Falmer, London and New York.

Edgar B and J Doherty, 2001, 'Supported Housing and Homelessness in the European Union', *European Journal of Housing Policy*, vol 1(1), pp 59–78.

Edwards, S, 2001, 'Domestic Violence and Homelessness: What are the Legal Parameters?', in *Out of the Fire: Domestic Violence and Homelessness*, Council to Homeless Persons, Melbourne.

Fischer, R, 2000, 'Towards Self-Sufficiency: Evaluating a Transitional Housing Program for Homeless Families', *Policy Studies Journal*, vol 28(2), pp 402–420.

Fitzpatrick, S, 2000, *Young Homeless People*, MacMillan, Basingstoke.

Giddens, A, 1979, *Central problems in social theory: Action, structure and contradiction in social analysis*, University of California Press, Berkeley.

Giddens, A, 1984, *The Constitution of society: Outline of the theory of structuration*, University of California Press, Berkeley.

Goffman, E, 1963, *Stigma: Notes on the Management of Spoiled Identity*, Penguin Books, Ringwood, Victoria.

Gregory, R, 2001, 'Revisiting Domestic Violence and Homelessness', in *Out of the Fire: Domestic Violence and Homelessness*, Council to Homeless Persons, Melbourne.

Grigsby, C, D Baumann, S Gregorich and C Roberts-Grey, 1990, 'Disaffiliation to Entrenchment: A Model for Understanding Homelessness', *Journal of Social Issues*, vol 46(4), pp 141–156.

Hallebone, E, 1997, 'Homelessness and Marginality in Australia: Young and Old People Excluded from Independence', in *Critical International Perspectives on Homelessness*, Praeger, Westport, Connecticut.

Hanover Welfare Services, 2006, 'Public Perceptions', Hanover Welfare Services, Melbourne.

Harter, L, C Berquist, S Titsworth, D Novak and T Brokaw, 2005, 'The Structuring of Invisibility Among the Hidden Homeless: The Politics of Space, Stigma, and Identity Construction', *Journal of Applied Communication Research*, vol 33(4), pp 305–327.

Harvey, C, H Evert , H Herrman, T Pinzone and O Gurele, 2002, 'Disability, homelessness and social relationships among people living with psychosis in Australia', *National Survey of Mental Health and Wellbeing Bulletin*, Commonwealth Department of Health and Ageing, Canberra.

Henderson, N, J Ross, S Darke, M Teesson and M Lynskey, 2002, 'Longitudinal studies of dependent heroin users in Australia: Feasibility and benefits', Monograph No. 49, National Drug and Alcohol Research Centre, University of New South Wales, Sydney.

Henderson, R, 1975, *Commission of Inquiry into Poverty, First Main Report*, Australian Government Publishing Service, Canberra.

Herman, D, E Susser, E Struening and B Link, 1997, 'Adverse Childhood Experiences: Are They Risk Factors for Adult Homelessness?', *American Journal of Public Health*, vol 87(2), pp 249–255.

Hier, S, P Korboot and R Schweitzer, 1990, 'Social adjustment and symptomology in two types of homeless adolescents: Runaways and throwaways', *Adolescence*, vol 25(100), pp 761–771.

Hirst, C, 1989, *Forced Exit: A Profile of the Young and Homeless in Inner Urban Melbourne*, The Salvation Army, Melbourne.

Hoch, C and R Slayton, 1989, *New Homelessness and Old: Community and the Skid Row Hotel*, Temple University Press, Philadelphia.

Hodder, T, M Teesson and N Buhrich, 1988, *Down and Out In Sydney: Prevalence of mental disorders, disability and health service use among homeless people in inner Sydney*, Sydney City Mission, Sydney.

Horn, M, 1999, *Drugs and Homelessness: The Prevalence of Alcohol and Drug Dependence among People experiencing Homelessness*, Hanover Welfare Services, Melbourne.

Horn, M and M Cooke, 2001, Hanover Family Outcomes Study: Profile of participating families and their experiences of homelessness, Hanover Welfare Services, Melbourne.

Horn, M, 2002, 'Increasing Homelessness: Evidence of housing market failure in Australia', *Just Policy*, vol 25, pp 26–31.

House of Representatives, 1995, *A Report on Aspects of Youth Homelessness*, Australian Government Publishing Service, Canberra.

Human Rights and Equal Opportunity Commission, 1989, *Our Homeless Children*, Australian Government Publishing Service, Canberra.

Huth, M, 1997, 'America's New Homeless', in *Critical International Perspectives on Homelessness*, Praeger, Westport, Connecticut.

Hutson, S and M Liddiard, 1994, *Youth Homelessness, The Construction of a Social Issue*, MacMillan, London.

Johnson, G, 2006, 'On the Move: A Longitudinal Study of Pathways In and Out of Homelessness', School of Global Studies, Social Science and Planning, RMIT University, Melbourne.

Jope, S, 2000, *On the threshold: The future of private rooming houses in the City of Yarra*, Brotherhood of St Laurence, Melbourne.

Kaufman, J and C Johnson, 2004, 'Stigmatised Individuals and the Process of Identity', *The Sociological Quarterly*, vol 45(4), pp 807–833.

Katz, M, 1993, 'The Urban Underclass as a Metaphor of Social Transformation', in *The Underclass Debate: Views from History*, Princeton University Press, Princeton, New Jersey.

Kennedy, C and S Fitzpatrick, 2001, 'Begging, Rough Sleeping and Social Exclusion: Implications for Social Policy', *Urban Studies*, vol 38(11), pp 2001–1016.

Koegel, P, 1992, 'Through a different lens: An anthropological perspective on the homeless mentally ill', *Culture, Medicine and Psychiatry* (Historical Archive) vol 16(1), pp 1–22.

Koegal, P, E Melamid and A Burnam, 1995, 'Childhood Risk Factors for Homelessness among Homeless Adults', *American Journal of Adolescent Health*, vol 85(12), pp 1624–1649.

La Gory, M, F Ritchey and K Fitzpatrick, 1991, 'Homelessness and Affiliation', *The Sociological Quarterly*, vol 32(2), pp 201–218.

Laing, L, 2000b, Progress, trends and challenges in Australian responses to domestic violence, Issues Paper 1, Australian Domestic and Family Violence Clearing House, NSW.

Laing, L, 2000a, Children, young people and domestic violence, Issues Paper 2, Australian Domestic Violence Clearing House, NSW.

Lawrence, C, 2001, 'Challenging Orthodoxies: The Next Step', in *Out of the Fire: Domestic Violence and Homelessness*, Council to Homeless Persons, Melbourne.

Leal, D, M Galanter, H Dermatis and L Westreich, 1998, 'Correlates of Protracted Homelessness in a Sample of Dually Diagnosed Psychiatric Inpatients', *Journal of Substance Abuse Treatment*, vol 16(2), pp 143–147.

Link, B, E Susser, A Stueve, J Phelan, R Moore and E Struening, 1994, 'Lifetime and Five-year Prevalence of Homelessness in the United States', *American Journal of Public Health*, vol 84(12).

Link, B and J Phelan, 2001, 'Conceptualizing Stigma', *American Review of Sociology*, vol 27, pp 363–385.

McCaughey, J, 1987, *A Bit of a Struggle: Coping with Family Life in Australia*, McPhee Gribble/Penguin Books, Melbourne.

McCaughey, J, 1991, 'Nomads in a settled population: Families and homelessness', Australian Institute of Family Studies, Melbourne.

McCaughey, J, 1992, 'Where now? A Study of Homeless Families in the 1990s', Australian Institute of Family Studies Policy Background Paper No. 8, Australian Institute of Family Studies, Melbourne.

McChesney, K, 1990, 'Family Homelessness: A Systemic Problem', *Journal of Social Issues*, vol 46(4), pp 191–205.

MacKenzie, D and C Chamberlain, 1995, 'The National Census of Homeless School Students', *Youth Studies Australia*, vol 14(1), pp22–28.

Mackenzie, D and C Chamberlain, 2003, *Homeless Careers: Pathways in and out of homelessness*, Swinburne and RMIT Universities, Melbourne.

McNaughton, C, 2005, Crossing the Continuum: 'Understanding routes out of Homelessness and examining "what works"', Simon Community, Glasgow.

Mallet, S, J Edwards, D Keys, P Myers and D Rosenthal, 2003, 'Disrupting Stereotypes: Young people, drug use and homelessness', Key Centre for Women's Health in Society, The University of Melbourne, Melbourne.

Marcuse, P, 1996, *Is Australia Different? Globalization and the New Urban Poverty*. Occasional Paper 3, Australian Housing and Research Institute, Melbourne.

Marks, R, 1989, 'Prohibition or Regulation: An Economist's View of Australian Heroin Policy', in *Fifth Annual Conference of the Australian and New Zealand Society of Criminology*, University of Sydney, New South Wales.

May, J, 2000, 'Housing Histories and Homeless Careers: A Biographical Approach', *Housing Studies*, vol 15(4), pp 613–638.

Meadowcroft, G and D Charman, 2000, 'A psychological study of young women', *The Australian Educational and Development Psychologist*, vol 17(2), pp 70–81.

Mendes, P and B Moslehuddin, 2004, 'Graduating from the child welfare system: a comparison of the UK and Australian leaving care debates', *International Journal of Social Welfare*, vol 13, pp 332–339.

Merton, R, 1968, *Social Theory and Social Structure*, The Free Press, New York.

Metraux, S and D Culhane, 1999, 'Family Dynamics, Housing and Recurring Homelessness Among Women in New York City Homeless Shelters', *Journal of Family Issues*, vol 20(3), pp 371–396.

Metraux, S and D Culhane, 2004, 'Homeless Shelter Use and Reincarceration Following Prison Release', *Criminology and Public Policy*, vol 3(2), pp 139–60.

Milburn, N, 1990, 'Drug Abuse among homeless people', in *Homelessness in the United States: Data and Issues*, Praeger, New York.

Miller, C and C Kaiser, 2001, 'A Theoretical Perspective on Coping with Stigma', *Journal of Social Issues*, vol 57(1), pp 73–92.

Momeni, J (ed.), 1990, *Homelessness in the United States – Data and Issues*, Praeger, New York.

Moore, D, 2004, 'Beyond "subculture" on the ethnography of illicit drug use', *Contemporary Drug Problems*, vol 31(2), pp 181–212.

Morrissey, J and D Dennis, 1990, 'Homelessness and mental illness: Toward the next generation of research studies', National Institute of Mental Health, Rockville MD.

Murray, S, 2002, *More than a Refuge: Changing Responses to Domestic Violence*, University of Western Australia Press, Perth.

National Committee for the Evaluation of the Youth Services Support Scheme, 1983, 'One step forward: Youth Homelessness and Emergency Accommodation Services', Australian Government Publishing Services, Canberra.

National Youth Coalition for Housing, 1999, 'Accommodating Homeless Young People with Mental Health Issues', National Research Project, Department of Family and Community Services, Canberra.

Neale, J, 2001, 'Homelessness amongst drug users: A double jeopardy explored', *The International Journal of Drug Policy*, vol 12, pp 353–369.

Neil, C and R Fopp, 1993, *Homelessness in Australia: Causes and Consequences*, CSIRO, Victorian Ministerial Advisory Committee on Homelessness and Housing.

NSW Ombudsman, 2004, 'Assisting homeless people – the need to improve their access to accommodation and support services', Final report arising from an Inquiry into access to, and exiting from, the Supported Accommodation Assistance Program, Sydney, New South Wales.

O'Connor, G, L Wurmser, T Brown and J Smith, 1972, 'The Economics of Heroin Addiction: A New Interpretation of the Facts', in *It's So Good, Don't Even Try It Once: Heroin in Perspective*, Prentice-Hall Inc, Englewood Cliffs, New Jersey.

O'Connor, I, 1989, *Our Homeless Children: Their Experiences*, 1989, Human Rights and Equal Opportunity Commission, Sydney.

O'Dwyer, B, 1997, 'Pathways to Homelessness: A Comparison of Gender and Schizophrenia in Inner-Sydney', *Australian Geographical Studies*, vol 35(3), pp 294–307.

O'Flaherty, B, 1996, *Making Room: The economics of homelessness*, Harvard University Press, Cambridge, Massachusetts.

Oyserman, D and J Swim, 2001, 'Stigma: An Insiders View', *Journal of Social Issues*, vol 57(1), pp 1–14.

Padgett, D, 2007, 'There's no place like (a) home: Ontological security among persons with a serious mental illness in the United States', *Social Science and Medicine*, vol 64, pp 1925–1936.

Padgett, D, L Gulcur and S Tsemberis, 2006, 'Housing First Services for People Who are Homeless With Co-Occurring Serious Mental Illness and Substance Abuse', *Research on Social Work*, vol 16(1), pp 74–83.

Phelan, J, B Link, R Moore and A Stueve, 1997, 'The stigma of homelessness: The impact of the label "Homelessness" on attitudes towards poor persons', *Social Psychology Quarterly*, vol 60(4), pp 323–337.

Phelan, J and B Link, 1999, 'Who are "the Homeless"? Reconsidering the Stability and Composition of the Homeless Population', *American Journal of Public Health*, vol 89(9).

Piliavin, I, H Westerfelt and E Elliott, 1989, 'Estimating Mental Illness among the Homeless: The Effects of Choice-Based Sampling', *Social Problems* vol 36(5).

Piliavin, I, M Sosin, A Westerfelt and R Matsueda, 1993, 'The Duration of Homeless Careers: An Exploratory Study', *Social Service Review*, vol 67(4), pp 576–598.

Piliavin, I, B Wright, R Mare and A Westerfelt, 1994, 'The Dynamics of Homelessness', Discussion Paper No. 1035-94, Institute for Research on Poverty, The University of Wisconsin-Madison.

Piliavin, I, B Wright, R Mare and A Westerfelt, 1996, 'Exits from and returns to Homelessness', *Social Service Review*, vol 70(1), pp 33–57.

Pinkey, S and S Ewing, 2006, 'The Costs and Pathways of Homelessness: Developing policy-relevant economic analyses for the Australian homelessness service system', Department of Families, Community Services and Indigenous Affairs, Canberra.

Randal, G, 1980, *No way Home: Homeless Young people in Central London*, Centrepoint Soho, London.

Rice, E, N Milburn, MJ Rotheram-Borus, S Mallett and D Rosenthal, 2005, 'The Effects of Peer Group Network Properties on Drug Use Among Homeless Youth', *American Behavioural Scientist*, vol 48(8), pp 613–638.

Robinson, C, 2003, 'Understanding iterative homelessness: The case of people with mental disorders, Australian Housing and Urban Research Institute', Melbourne.

Roman N and P Wolfe, 1997, 'The Relationship between Foster Care and Homelessness', *Public Welfare*, vol 55(1).

Roschelle, A and P Kaufman, 2004, 'Fitting In and Fighting Back: Stigma Management Strategies among Homeless Kids', *Symbolic Interaction*, vol 27(1), p 23.

Rossi, P, 1989, *Down and Out in America: The Origins of Homelessness*, 1989, Chicago University Press, Chicago.

Rossiter, B, S Mallett, P Myers and D Rosenthal, 2003, 'Living Well? Homeless young people in Melbourne', Australian Research Centre in Sex, Health and Society, Melbourne.

Rowe, J, 2002a, 'Heroin epidemic! Drugs and the moral panic in the western suburbs of Melbourne', *Just Policy*, vol 27, pp 38–45.

Rowe, J, 2002b, 'Survival Strategies of the Homeless and Drug Dependent', in *Housing, Crime and Stronger Communities Conference*, Australian Institute of Criminology and Australian Housing and Urban Research Institute, Melbourne.

RPR Consulting, 2002, Making a Difference: First Report of the Longitudinal Evaluation of Reconnect.

Salins, P, 2006, *The Concise Encyclopedia of Economics*, D Henderson (ed.), econlib.org/library/Enc/Housing.html

Saunders, P, 2002, *The Ends and Means of Welfare: Coping with Economic and Social Change in Australia*, Cambridge University Press, Cambridge.

Saunders, P, 2004, *Australia's welfare habit and how to kick it*, Centre for Independent Studies, St Leonards, New South Wales.

Saunders, P, Y Naidoo and M Griffiths, 2007, Towards New Indicators of Disadvantage: Deprivation and Social Exclusion in Australia, Social Policy Research Centre, University of New South Wales.

Shih, M, 2004, 'Positive Stigma: Examining Resilience and Empowerment in Overcoming Stigma', *The Annals of the American Academy*, vol 591 (January), pp 175–185.

Shlay, A and P Rossi, 1992, 'Social Science Research and Contemporary Studies of Homelessness', *Annual Review of Sociology*, vol 18, pp 129–160.

Smith, J, 1995, *Being young and homeless*, The Salvation Army, Melbourne.

Snow, D and L Anderson, 1993, *Down on their Luck: A study of homeless street people*, University of California Press, Berkeley.

Snow, D, S Baker and L Anderson, 1989, 'Criminality and Homeless Men: An Empirical Assessment', *Social Problems*, vol 36(5), pp 532–549.

Sosin, M, I Piliavin and H Westerfelt, 1990, 'Toward a Longitudinal Analysis of Homelessness', *Journal of Social Issues*, vol 46(4), pp 157–174.

Susser, E, E Valencia, S Conover, A Felix, WY Tsai and RJ Wyatt, 1997, 'Preventing Recurrent Homelessness among Mentally Ill Men: A "Critical Time" Intervention after Discharge from a Shelter', *American Journal of Public Health*, vol 87(2), pp 256–262.

Sykes, H, 1993, *Youth Homelessness: Courage and Hope*, Melbourne University Press, Melbourne.

Teeson, M, T Hodder and N Buhrich, 2000, 'Substance abuse disorders among homeless people in inner Sydney', *Social Psychiatry*, vol 35, pp 451–456.

Thompson Goodall and Associates, 1999a, 'Understanding Demand for Crisis Accommodation: A Snapshot Analysis of Current Demand on Major Crisis Accommodation Services in Inner Urban Melbourne', Melbourne.

Thompson Goodall and Associates, Pty Ltd, 1999b, 'Early Intervention in SAAP: A report prepared for the Department of Family and Community Services', DFACS, Canberra.

Tosi, A, 2005, 'Rehousing and Social Integration of Homeless People: A case study from Milan', *Innovation: The European Journal of Social Science Research*, vol 18(2), pp 183–203.

Tracy, E and R Stoecker, 1993, 'Homelessness: The Service Providers' Perspective on Victim Blaming', *Journal of Sociology and Social Welfare*, vol 20(3), pp 43–59.

Tsemberis, S, 1999, 'From Streets to Homes: An Innovative Approach to Supported Housing for Homeless Adults with Psychiatric Disabilities', *Journal of Community Psychology*, vol 27(2), pp 225–241.

Tsemberis, S, L Gulcur and M Nakae, 2004, 'Housing First, Consumer Choice, and Harm Reduction for Homeless Individuals With a Dual Diagnosis', *American Journal of Public Health*, vol 94(4), pp 651–656.

Twaite, J and D Lampert, 1997, 'Outcomes of mandated preventative services programs for homeless and truant children: A follow-up study', *Social Work*, vol 41(1), pp 11–18.

Victorian Government, 1992, Making a Difference: A Progress Report on Youth Homelessness, Victorian Government, Melbourne.

Victorian Homelessness Strategy, 2002, Action Plan and Strategic Framework: Directions for Change – A collaborative approach to improving our response to homelessness, Department of Human Services, Melbourne.

Vissing, Y 1990, Out of Sight, *Out of Mind: Homeless Children and Families in Small-town America*, The University Press of Kentucky, Kentucky.

Wagner, D, 1997, 'Reinterpreting the "Undeserving Poor": From Pathology to Resistance', in *International Critical Perspectives on Homelessness*, Praeger, New York.

Wallace, R and E Bassuk, 1991, 'Housing famine and homelessness: how the low income housing crisis affects families with inadequate supports', *Environment and Planning*, vol 23, pp 485–498.

Wallace, S, 1965, *Skid row as a way of life*, Bedminster Press, Totowa, NJ.

Watson, S, 2001, 'Homelessness Revisited: New Reflections on Old Paradigms', *Urban Policy and Research*, vol 82(2), pp 159–170.

Westerfelt, H, 1990, 'The ins and outs of homelessness: Exit patterns and predictions', in *Graduate School – Social Welfare*, University of Wisconsin, Ann Arbor.

Wolch, J, M Dear and A Akita, 1998, 'Explaining Homelessness', *Journal of the American Planning Association*, vol 54(4), pp 443–454.

Wong, I, 1997, 'Patterns of Homelessness: A Review of Longitudinal Studies', in *Understanding Homelessness: New policy and Research Perspectives*, Fannie Mae Foundation, Washington DC.

Wong, I, D Culhane and R Kuhn, 1997, 'Predictors of Exit and Reentry among Homeless Family Shelter Users in New York City', *Social Service Review*, vol 74(3), pp 441–462.

Wong, I and I Piliavin, 1997, 'A Dynamic Analysis of Homeless-Domicile Transitions', *Social Problems*, vol 44(3), pp 408–423.

Wright, B, A Caspi, T Moffitt and P Silvia, 1998, 'Factors Associated with Doubled-Up Housing: A Common Precursor to Homelessness', *Social Service Review*, vol 72(1), pp 92–111.

Wright-Howie, D, 2004, 'Public Housing in Australia is in Decline: The Facts Speak for Themselves', *Parity*, vol 17(10).

Yates, J and G Wood, 2005, 'Affordable Rental Housing: Lost, Stolen and Strayed', *The Economic Record*, vol 81(255) pp 82–95.

Yates, J and M Gabriel, 2006, Housing affordability in Australia, National Research Venture 3: Housing affordability for lower income Australians, Australian Housing and Urban Research Institute, Melbourne.

Zlotnick, C, D Kronstadt and L Klee, 1998, 'Foster Care Children and Family Homelessness', *American Journal of Public Health*, vol 88 (9).

Zlotnick, C, M Robertson and M Lahiff, 1999, 'Getting off the Streets: Economic Resources and Residential Exits from Homelessness', *Journal of Community Psychology*, vol 27(2), pp 209–224.

INDEX